CALEB ROSS

Scalable AWS cloud Architecture

Contents

Introduction

C loud computing has transformed the way businesses operate, enabling rapid innovation, scalability, and cost efficiency. The demand for scalable solutions is growing exponentially as companies increasingly rely on digital platforms to serve customers globally. A scalable cloud architecture allows businesses to handle unpredictable workloads and user demands without sacrificing performance or user experience.

This book, *"Scalable AWS Cloud Architecture,"* is designed to help readers understand the principles of building scalable, resilient, and cost-effective solutions using Amazon Web Services (AWS). Whether you are a cloud architect, developer, or IT professional, this book provides practical guidance, hands-on examples, and insights into AWS tools and services that facilitate scalable architecture design.

In this chapter, we will:

1. Discuss the concept of scalability and its importance in cloud computing.
2. Explore why AWS is a popular choice for building scalable architectures.
3. Identify key challenges that organizations face when achieving scalability.
4. Provide an overview of what this book covers to help you succeed in implementing scalable cloud architectures.

Overview of Cloud Scalability

Understanding Scalability in Cloud Computing

Scalability is the capability of a system, network, or process to handle increasing amounts of work, or its potential to accommodate growth. In cloud computing, scalability is a crucial attribute because it determines how well your applications can grow to meet demand. Scalability can be categorized into two main types:

1. **Vertical Scalability (Scaling Up):** Involves increasing the capacity of a single resource, such as upgrading a server's CPU, memory, or storage. For example, you might scale a database instance from a smaller instance type to a larger one with more CPU and RAM.
2. **Horizontal Scalability (Scaling Out):** Involves adding more instances or nodes to distribute the workload. For example, adding multiple servers to distribute web traffic or implementing a load-balanced architecture.

In the context of cloud computing, horizontal scalability is often the preferred choice because it allows systems to handle large, distributed workloads effectively. AWS provides a vast array of services that support both horizontal and vertical scaling, enabling users to choose the best approach based on their application requirements.

Why Scalability is Critical

Modern applications face unpredictable user demand, especially during events like product launches, sales promotions, or viral trends. A well-architected scalable solution ensures that your applications can automatically adjust to changing loads without any downtime or degraded performance. Some of the benefits of scalability include:

- **Improved User Experience:** Scalable applications can handle traffic spikes, ensuring smooth user interactions.
- **Cost Efficiency:** AWS allows you to scale up or down based on demand,

which helps reduce costs by avoiding overprovisioning.

- **Global Reach:** With scalable cloud solutions, businesses can expand their services to users worldwide without worrying about infrastructure limitations.

The Role of Cloud Computing in Scalability

Before the advent of cloud computing, scalability was limited by the constraints of physical hardware. Companies had to purchase and maintain servers, leading to excessive capital expenditure and limited flexibility. However, cloud computing platforms like AWS revolutionized scalability by offering virtualized, elastic infrastructure.

Key features of cloud computing that enable scalability:

1. **On-Demand Resources:** Cloud platforms offer on-demand compute, storage, and networking resources, eliminating the need for up-front investments.
2. **Elasticity:** Cloud solutions provide the ability to automatically adjust resource allocation based on demand, making it easier to scale applications.
3. **Pay-as-You-Go:** With cloud providers like AWS, you only pay for the resources you use, which makes it economically viable to scale applications as needed.

Why AWS for Scalable Architecture?

Amazon Web Services (AWS) is the leading cloud service provider, offering a comprehensive suite of services and tools designed for building scalable architectures. There are several reasons why AWS stands out as the go-to platform for designing scalable cloud solutions:

1. Comprehensive Service Offerings

AWS offers over 200 services that cater to various aspects of cloud computing, including compute, storage, networking, databases, security, and machine learning. These services are specifically designed to work together seamlessly, making it easier to build, deploy, and manage scalable solutions.

- **Elastic Compute Cloud (EC2):** Provides resizable compute capacity with options for various instance types, including general-purpose, memory-optimized, and compute-optimized instances.
- **Elastic Load Balancing (ELB):** Distributes incoming traffic across multiple targets, ensuring high availability and fault tolerance.
- **Auto Scaling:** Allows you to automatically scale EC2 instances based on defined policies and thresholds, ensuring that your application can handle varying workloads.
- **Amazon RDS and DynamoDB:** Offer scalable database solutions for both relational and NoSQL use cases.

2. Global Infrastructure and Availability

AWS boasts a global network of data centers spread across multiple regions and availability zones. This global infrastructure enables businesses to build resilient applications that can serve users from different geographic locations with low latency. AWS offers:

- **Availability Zones (AZs):** Multiple, isolated data centers within each region to ensure high availability and disaster recovery capabilities.
- **Edge Locations:** AWS has over 400 edge locations worldwide, enabling low-latency content delivery through services like Amazon CloudFront.

3. Flexibility and Elasticity

AWS provides unparalleled flexibility in terms of service choices and configurations. Whether you need serverless computing with AWS Lambda, container-based deployments with ECS or EKS, or traditional EC2 instances, AWS offers the right solution to meet your scalability requirements. Elasticity features in AWS enable applications to automatically adjust resources based on demand.

- **Elastic Load Balancing:** Distributes traffic efficiently across multiple instances to ensure high availability.

- **Amazon CloudWatch and Auto Scaling:** Allow you to monitor applications and scale resources automatically based on custom-defined metrics.

4. Pay-as-You-Go Pricing Model

AWS's pricing model allows you to only pay for the resources you use, which makes it economically feasible to implement scalable architectures. Businesses can start small, and as their requirements grow, AWS allows them to scale without committing to large upfront costs. This flexibility encourages experimentation and growth.

5. Security and Compliance

Scalability should not compromise security. AWS has a comprehensive suite of security tools and services that enable users to build secure, scalable solutions. From Identity and Access Management (IAM) to Virtual Private Cloud (VPC) configurations, AWS provides several ways to secure cloud applications and meet compliance requirements.

Key Challenges in Achieving Scalability

While AWS offers all the necessary tools and services to build scalable architectures, achieving scalability is not without challenges. Here are some common hurdles:

1. Designing Efficiently for Horizontal Scalability

Scaling out is not just about adding more servers; it requires an architectural approach that can handle distributed workloads, data consistency, and effective load distribution. Designing applications to work efficiently in a distributed environment can be challenging, particularly when it involves synchronizing state across multiple instances or regions.

- **Challenge:** Building stateless applications and handling session management.
- **Solution:** Using services like ElastiCache for session storage and

leveraging serverless technologies like AWS Lambda.

2. Managing Costs While Scaling

As applications grow, costs can spiral out of control if not properly managed. Efficient cost management involves understanding the trade-offs between different AWS services and choosing the right instance types, storage solutions, and scaling policies.

- **Challenge:** Balancing cost optimization with performance and user experience.
- **Solution:** Utilizing cost monitoring tools like AWS Cost Explorer and leveraging spot instances or savings plans.

3. Ensuring Security in a Scalable Environment

Security is often an afterthought, but it must be integrated into the architecture from the start. With scalable architectures, ensuring consistent security policies across distributed components becomes more complex.

- **Challenge:** Managing access control and network security in large-scale environments.
- **Solution:** Implementing IAM policies, using VPC security groups, and encrypting data with AWS KMS.

4. Dealing with Regional Failover and High Availability

Building highly available architectures that can withstand failures in specific regions or data centers requires careful planning. Multi-region architectures must address challenges related to data consistency, latency, and cross-region replication.

- **Challenge:** Implementing cross-region replication and handling failover without affecting user experience.
- **Solution:** Utilizing services like Amazon Aurora Global Databases and Amazon Route 53 for DNS-based failover.

5. Performance Optimization and Latency Reduction

As applications scale, latency issues can impact user experience, especially in geographically distributed systems. Optimizing network latency, database access, and content delivery becomes essential.

- **Challenge:** Reducing latency in global applications.
- **Solution:** Implementing edge caching with Amazon CloudFront and optimizing VPC configurations for data transfer.

What This Book Covers

This book aims to provide a comprehensive guide to designing, implementing, and optimizing scalable architectures on AWS. It is structured to cater to both beginners and experienced cloud architects, covering essential topics like scalability principles, service comparisons, best practices, and advanced architectural patterns.

What You Will Learn:

1. **Fundamentals of Scalable Cloud Architecture:** An introduction to scalability principles, including horizontal and vertical scaling, and an overview of key AWS services that enable scalable solutions.
2. **Hands-On Guides to Building Scalable Applications:** Practical, step-by-step tutorials for designing scalable web applications, microservices, serverless architectures, and more using AWS tools.
3. **Advanced Strategies for Cost Optimization, Security, and High Availability:** Best practices for balancing cost, performance, and security in scalable AWS architectures.
4. **Future-Proofing Your Architecture:** Insights into emerging trends, technologies, and future considerations for maintaining scalable solutions in the cloud.
5. **Real-World Case Studies:** Detailed analysis of how businesses have successfully implemented scalable solutions using AWS.

Book Structure

The book is divided into several chapters, each focusing on a specific aspect of scalability:

- **Chapter 1** introduces the fundamentals of scalable architecture and AWS services.
- **Chapters 2 to 4** cover hands-on guides for building various scalable solutions, including web applications, serverless architectures, and microservices.
- **Chapters 5 to 8** delve into advanced topics such as cost management, security, multi-region deployment, and networking.
- **Chapter 9** explores AI and ML scalability using AWS services like SageMaker.
- **Chapters 10 to 12** discuss monitoring, optimization, and future-proofing.
- **Chapter 13** presents real-world case studies to solidify concepts.
- **Chapters 14 to 15** conclude the book with a recap and forward-looking insights.

Who This Book Is For:

This book is designed for cloud architects, developers, IT professionals, and anyone interested in learning about scalable cloud solutions using AWS. It is equally valuable for beginners who are getting started with cloud architecture and experienced professionals looking to deepen their understanding of scalability in AWS.

Why This Book Stands Out:

- **Comprehensive Coverage:** Covers both fundamental and advanced scalability concepts, tools, and techniques.
- **Practical Focus:** Hands-on examples, templates, and blueprints for real-world implementations.
- **Advanced Insights:** Best practices for optimizing costs, improving performance, and ensuring security.

- **Real-World Case Studies:** Detailed analysis of real-world architectures for various industries and use cases.

By following this introductory guide, readers will have a solid understanding of cloud scalability, why AWS is a preferred platform, and the key challenges to consider when designing scalable architectures. The subsequent chapters will build on these fundamentals, providing detailed, practical guidance on implementing scalable solutions using AWS.

Chapter 1: Fundamentals of Scalable Cloud Architecture

1. Principles of Scalability

1.1 Defining Scalability in Cloud Computing

Scalability refers to the ability of a system or application to handle an increasing amount of work, or its potential to accommodate growth. In cloud architecture, scalability is crucial because it directly impacts performance, user experience, and business growth. Scalability is about making systems adaptable, efficient, and resilient in response to workload demands. There are two primary types of scalability:

- **Vertical Scalability (Scaling Up):** This involves adding more resources (like CPU, memory, or storage) to a single machine. For example, increasing an EC2 instance size from a small instance to a larger one.
- **Horizontal Scalability (Scaling Out):** This involves adding more instances of a resource to distribute the load. For example, adding more web servers behind a load balancer to handle increasing web traffic.

Both of these types of scalability have their use cases and limitations. Horizontal scaling is typically preferred in cloud computing environments like AWS due to its fault tolerance, flexibility, and the ability to distribute the load across multiple resources.

1.2 Characteristics of Scalable Systems

Scalable systems are designed with several key characteristics in mind:

- **Elasticity:** The ability to dynamically adjust resources based on current demand. Elasticity helps to optimize cost and maintain performance by automatically scaling resources up or down.
- **Modularity:** Scalable systems are modular, making it easier to add or remove components without disrupting the entire system.
- **Statelessness:** Stateless applications simplify horizontal scaling because each instance can handle any incoming request without maintaining session information.
- **Asynchronous Communication:** Using asynchronous methods for communication between services enables better handling of large, concurrent workloads.

1.3 Patterns of Scalable Cloud Architecture

Several architectural patterns are crucial for building scalable systems. These include:

- **Microservices Architecture:** Dividing a monolithic application into smaller, independent services that can be developed, deployed, and scaled separately. This pattern is common in large-scale, cloud-native applications.
- **Serverless Architecture:** Leveraging serverless computing services like AWS Lambda to build scalable applications without managing servers.
- **Distributed Systems:** Distributing tasks and data across multiple servers and locations to ensure scalability, availability, and fault tolerance.
- **Event-Driven Architecture:** Utilizing an event-driven approach allows applications to react to events in real-time, enhancing scalability and responsiveness.

2. AWS Infrastructure Essentials

2.1 Introduction to AWS Global Infrastructure

AWS offers a robust, secure, and globally distributed infrastructure, which is critical for building scalable cloud architectures. AWS infrastructure is divided into several key components:

- **Regions and Availability Zones (AZs):** AWS Regions are geographic locations, and each Region contains multiple isolated data centers known as Availability Zones. This allows for fault-tolerant architectures, with each AZ serving as an independent failure domain.
- **Edge Locations:** AWS has over 400 edge locations globally, which serve as distribution points for content delivery through services like Amazon CloudFront. This reduces latency for users worldwide and enhances scalability.

2.2 Amazon Elastic Compute Cloud (EC2)

EC2 is a core component of AWS that provides resizable compute capacity. It forms the backbone of most scalable AWS architectures. Key features of EC2 related to scalability include:

- **Instance Types:** AWS offers a wide range of EC2 instance types to suit various workloads, including general-purpose, compute-optimized, memory-optimized, and GPU instances.
- **Elastic IP Addresses:** Static, scalable IP addresses that you can associate with EC2 instances.
- **Elastic Block Store (EBS):** Scalable block storage volumes that can be attached to EC2 instances for data persistence.

2.3 Virtual Private Cloud (VPC)

VPC enables you to create logically isolated networks in the AWS cloud. It provides essential networking components that support scalable architectures:

12

- **Subnets:** Allow you to segment your VPC into smaller networks. You can configure public subnets for internet-facing resources and private subnets for backend services.
- **Route Tables and Gateways:** Enable communication within and outside your VPC.
- **VPC Peering and Transit Gateway:** Facilitate scalable and secure communication between different VPCs, enabling multi-region architectures.

2.4 Amazon Simple Storage Service (S3)

S3 is a highly scalable object storage service. It's a key component in scalable architectures due to its ability to store and retrieve vast amounts of data with low latency. Features that make S3 suitable for scalability include:

- **Object Versioning and Lifecycle Policies:** Allow you to manage data growth efficiently by archiving or deleting old versions of objects.
- **S3 Cross-Region Replication:** Enables the automatic replication of data across AWS Regions, which is crucial for building fault-tolerant and globally scalable architectures.
- **S3 Glacier and S3 Glacier Deep Archive:** Provide cost-effective, scalable solutions for data archiving.

3. Understanding Load Balancing and Auto Scaling

3.1 The Role of Load Balancing in Scalability

Load balancing is the distribution of incoming network traffic across multiple servers. In scalable architectures, load balancers are essential for achieving high availability and fault tolerance. AWS offers multiple load balancing solutions:

- **Elastic Load Balancer (ELB):** Automatically distributes incoming traffic across multiple targets, such as EC2 instances, containers, and IP addresses.
- **Application Load Balancer (ALB):** Ideal for HTTP/HTTPS traffic and

provides advanced routing features.

- **Network Load Balancer (NLB):** Handles TCP traffic and offers ultra-low latency.
- **Gateway Load Balancer (GWLB):** Allows you to deploy, scale, and manage virtual appliances, such as firewalls and network monitoring tools.

3.2 How Load Balancers Improve Scalability and Availability

Load balancers enhance scalability by distributing workloads across multiple instances, thus preventing any single instance from becoming a bottleneck. Some key benefits include:

- **High Availability:** If one instance fails, traffic is automatically rerouted to healthy instances.
- **Efficient Traffic Distribution:** Traffic is balanced based on pre-defined rules and algorithms, such as round-robin, least connections, or IP hash.
- **Advanced Health Checks:** Load balancers continuously monitor target instances and automatically remove unhealthy instances from the pool.

3.3 Introduction to Auto Scaling

Auto Scaling allows you to automatically adjust the number of EC2 instances in your application based on demand. This ensures that you have the right amount of capacity to handle the load efficiently. AWS provides two primary types of Auto Scaling:

- **EC2 Auto Scaling:** Dynamically adjusts the number of EC2 instances based on scaling policies and alarms.
- **Application Auto Scaling:** Supports other AWS services like DynamoDB, ECS, and Lambda, allowing them to scale automatically.

3.4 Configuring Auto Scaling Policies

When setting up Auto Scaling, it's essential to define policies that dictate when and how scaling occurs. Key components include:

- **Scaling Policies:** Determine how the system should respond to metrics. These include target tracking, step scaling, and scheduled scaling.
- **CloudWatch Alarms:** Monitor specific metrics such as CPU utilization, memory usage, or network traffic. When a threshold is breached, an alarm triggers an Auto Scaling action.
- **Launch Configurations and Templates:** Define the specifications for new instances, such as instance type, AMI, and security groups.

4. Key AWS Services for Scalability

4.1 Amazon Elastic Kubernetes Service (EKS)

Amazon EKS is a managed Kubernetes service that allows you to run and scale containerized applications using Kubernetes. It provides automated updates, monitoring, and high availability, making it a popular choice for scalable container orchestration. Key features include:

- **Cluster Auto Scaling:** Dynamically scales your Kubernetes clusters based on workload requirements.
- **Integration with AWS Services:** EKS integrates with services like ALB, CloudWatch, and IAM, simplifying the deployment of scalable applications.

4.2 AWS Lambda and Serverless Scalability

AWS Lambda is a serverless compute service that automatically scales your code in response to incoming requests or events. It abstracts server management, allowing you to focus solely on your application logic. Some benefits of AWS Lambda include:

- **Automatic Scaling:** AWS Lambda scales horizontally by running multiple instances of your function in parallel.
- **Event-Driven Architecture:** You can trigger Lambda functions using various AWS services like S3, DynamoDB, and SNS, making it suitable for real-time and asynchronous processing.

- **Pay-As-You-Go:** You only pay for the compute time used by your functions, making Lambda a cost-effective solution for unpredictable workloads.

4.3 Amazon DynamoDB for Scalable Databases

DynamoDB is a fully managed NoSQL database service designed for fast, consistent performance at any scale. It supports flexible data models, making it ideal for various use cases. Key features include:

- **On-Demand and Provisioned Capacity Modes:** Allow you to choose between pre-allocated capacity or automatically adjusting based on demand.
- **Global Tables:** Support multi-region replication, enabling you to build globally distributed applications with low-latency access.
- **DynamoDB Streams:** Allow you to capture changes to DynamoDB tables and trigger actions using AWS Lambda.

4.4 Amazon S3 and CloudFront for Content Delivery

Amazon S3 is a highly scalable object storage service, while Amazon CloudFront is a global content delivery network (CDN). Together, they form a powerful combination for storing and delivering content at scale. Features that enhance scalability include:

- **S3 Lifecycle Policies:** Automatically transition objects between different storage classes based on pre-defined rules, optimizing costs while scaling storage.
- **CloudFront Edge Locations:** Deliver content with low latency to users around the world, improving performance and scalability.

4.5 Amazon RDS and Aurora for Relational Databases

Amazon RDS and Amazon Aurora provide scalable, managed database solutions for relational workloads. Key features related to scalability include:

- **Read Replicas:** Allow you to create multiple read-only copies of your database to offload read-heavy workloads.
- **Aurora Serverless:** Automatically scales database capacity based on demand, eliminating the need for manual scaling.
- **Multi-AZ Deployments:** Enable automatic failover to a standby replica in case of an outage, ensuring high availability.

Conclusion

Chapter 1 provides a comprehensive foundation in understanding scalable cloud architecture on AWS. The concepts and services discussed here—principles of scalability, essential AWS infrastructure, load balancing, auto scaling, and key AWS services—serve as the building blocks for the rest of the book. This chapter sets the stage for more advanced topics, real-world applications, and hands-on guides to building and optimizing scalable solutions in AWS.

Chapter 2: Building Scalable Web Applications

Overview

Web applications are at the heart of most digital transformations. From e-commerce platforms to social networks, scalable web applications allow businesses to grow without compromising user experience. In this chapter, we will explore the architectural patterns, best practices, and AWS services that enable building scalable and resilient web applications.

1. Understanding Scalable Web Applications

1.1 Characteristics of a Scalable Web Application

A scalable web application can handle increasing traffic and data volumes without degrading performance. Key characteristics include:

- **Modularity:** Breaking down an application into separate modules or components that can be scaled independently.
- **Stateless Design:** Stateless applications can scale horizontally more efficiently as each instance can handle any incoming request.

- **Efficient Data Caching:** Using caching strategies to reduce the load on databases and improve response times.
- **Distributed Processing:** Distributing the workload across multiple servers or nodes to ensure balanced performance.

1.2 The Role of Distributed Systems in Scalability

Scalable web applications often rely on distributed systems to handle large volumes of traffic and data. Distributed systems enhance scalability through:

- **Load Distribution:** Distributing incoming requests across multiple servers.
- **Data Partitioning:** Dividing large datasets into smaller, manageable partitions.
- **Failure Tolerance:** Isolating failures to prevent disruptions in the entire system.

2. Designing Multi-Tier Architectures

2.1 The Basics of Multi-Tier Architecture

A multi-tier architecture separates an application into distinct layers, each responsible for a specific set of functions. Common tiers include:

- **Presentation Tier (Front-End):** Handles user interfaces and user interactions. This tier typically uses HTML, CSS, JavaScript, or front-end frameworks like React or Angular.
- **Application Tier (Back-End):** Processes business logic, data manipulation, and integrations. The application tier usually consists of server-side code running on web servers.
- **Database Tier:** Stores and manages persistent data. Common choices include relational databases like Amazon RDS or NoSQL databases like DynamoDB.

2.2 Implementing Load Balancing and Caching Layers

Effective multi-tier architectures use load balancing and caching to enhance scalability and performance. Considerations include:

- **Load Balancing at the Application Tier:** Using an AWS Application Load Balancer (ALB) to distribute incoming traffic evenly across multiple EC2 instances or containers.
- **Caching at Multiple Tiers:** Leveraging services like Amazon Cloud-Front and AWS ElastiCache to cache static and dynamic content at the front-end and application layers.
- **Database Replication and Caching:** Implementing read replicas in Amazon RDS to offload read-heavy operations and using ElastiCache to cache frequently accessed data.

2.3 Security Considerations in Multi-Tier Architectures

Scalable applications should also be secure by design. Key security measures include:

- **Segregating Public and Private Subnets:** Hosting front-end components in public subnets and back-end databases in private subnets to limit external access.
- **Using Security Groups and Network ACLs:** Defining firewall rules to control inbound and outbound traffic between tiers.
- **Securing Data in Transit:** Encrypting data transmitted between different application tiers using SSL/TLS.

3. Leveraging Serverless Components in Web Applications

3.1 Introduction to Serverless Architectures

Serverless computing abstracts server management tasks, allowing developers to focus on application logic. AWS Lambda is at the core of serverless architectures. It automatically scales the number of function instances in response to incoming requests.

3.2 Building a Serverless Web Application

A typical serverless web application architecture on AWS consists of:

- **AWS Lambda:** For processing business logic and events.
- **Amazon API Gateway:** Acts as a front door for routing HTTP requests to Lambda functions.
- **Amazon DynamoDB:** Serves as a scalable NoSQL database for storing application data.
- **Amazon S3 and CloudFront:** Host static assets like HTML, CSS, and JavaScript, while CloudFront provides CDN-based caching for faster delivery.

3.3 Benefits and Challenges of Serverless Web Applications
Benefits:

- **Automatic Scaling:** Lambda functions scale automatically based on incoming requests, reducing the need for manual intervention.
- **Cost Efficiency:** Pay-per-use pricing for Lambda functions means you only pay for the compute time consumed.

Challenges:

- **Cold Start Latency:** Occasionally, serverless functions experience cold start latency when scaled from zero. Solutions include using provisioned concurrency for critical functions.

4. Optimizing Database Performance for Scalability

4.1 Choosing the Right Database Solution
Selecting the right database for your application is crucial. Factors to consider include:

- **Data Consistency and Transactions:** If strong consistency is essential, use a relational database like Amazon RDS. For eventual consistency,

NoSQL databases like DynamoDB might be more suitable.

- **Read and Write Scaling Requirements:** DynamoDB offers fine-grained control over read and write throughput, which is essential for applications with varying demand.

4.2 Implementing Read Replicas and Multi-AZ Deployments

Amazon RDS supports read replicas and Multi-AZ deployments to improve scalability and availability:

- **Read Replicas:** Create read replicas to offload read-heavy workloads from the master database.
- **Multi-AZ Deployments:** Replicate databases across Availability Zones for fault tolerance.

4.3 Leveraging Caching for Enhanced Performance

Incorporate caching mechanisms like ElastiCache to reduce latency and improve database performance. Common strategies include:

- **Lazy Loading:** Load and cache data only when requested, with cache misses being fetched from the database.
- **Write-Through:** Update the cache immediately when the database is updated, ensuring cache consistency.

5. Managing Large-Scale Data with AWS S3 and RDS

5.1 Data Storage Strategies for Scalability

For scalable applications, consider a data storage strategy that aligns with your use case:

- **Object Storage with S3:** Ideal for storing unstructured or semi-structured data like media files, logs, and backups.
- **Relational Storage with RDS:** Use RDS for transactional data that requires strong consistency and complex querying.

- **NoSQL Storage with DynamoDB:** Ideal for applications requiring high throughput and low-latency access to key-value data.

5.2 Best Practices for Managing Data in AWS

To manage large-scale data effectively:

- **Lifecycle Policies:** Automate data management by moving older objects to cheaper storage classes like S3 Glacier.
- **Data Compression:** Reduce storage costs and improve performance by compressing large datasets before storing them in S3.

6. Implementing Asynchronous Processing and Event-Driven Workloads

6.1 Introduction to Asynchronous Processing

Asynchronous processing enables applications to handle large volumes of tasks without blocking the main processing flow. This is critical for web applications with tasks like batch processing, image resizing, and report generation.

6.2 Using AWS SQS and SNS for Asynchronous Processing

AWS offers Simple Queue Service (SQS) and Simple Notification Service (SNS) to facilitate asynchronous workflows:

- **SQS:** A fully managed message queuing service that decouples and distributes tasks across multiple components.
- **SNS:** A messaging service that allows you to publish messages to multiple subscribers, including Lambda functions, email endpoints, and mobile push notifications.

6.3 Implementing Real-Time Processing with AWS Kinesis

For applications that require real-time data streaming and processing, AWS Kinesis is an ideal choice. Key features include:

- **Kinesis Data Streams:** Allow you to ingest and process real-time data at scale.
- **Kinesis Firehose:** Provides a simple way to deliver streaming data to AWS destinations like S3, Redshift, and Elasticsearch.

7. Monitoring and Managing Scalable Web Applications

7.1 Setting Up Monitoring and Alerts with Amazon CloudWatch

CloudWatch enables you to monitor AWS resources and applications effectively. Key monitoring practices include:

- **Setting Up Metrics and Dashboards:** Monitor essential metrics like CPU utilization, latency, request count, and error rates.
- **Creating Alarms and Automated Actions:** Configure CloudWatch Alarms to trigger automated actions like scaling events, SNS notifications, or Lambda functions.

7.2 Performance Tuning for Scalable Web Applications

Continuously monitor and optimize the performance of your web application by:

- **Optimizing Code and Database Queries:** Regularly review and optimize inefficient code paths or database queries to reduce latency.
- **Using Auto Scaling Policies:** Implement Auto Scaling policies based on real-time monitoring data to ensure adequate capacity during peak times.

8. Case Study: Building a Scalable E-commerce Platform on AWS

8.1 Overview of the Use Case

This section will provide a detailed case study of designing and implementing a scalable e-commerce platform on AWS. The key requirements include handling traffic spikes during promotional events, managing large volumes of data, and ensuring a seamless user experience.

8.2 Architectural Design and Key Decisions

Explain the architecture for the scalable e-commerce platform, including:

- **Front-End:** Hosted on Amazon S3 and served through Amazon Cloud-Front.
- **Application Tier:** Built using EC2 Auto Scaling groups behind an Application Load Balancer.
- **Database Layer:** Utilizes Amazon RDS for transactional data and DynamoDB for high-throughput read and write operations.
- **Asynchronous Workflows:** Handles background tasks like order processing using AWS SQS and Lambda functions.

8.3 Implementation and Best Practices

Detail the implementation process, including:

- **Deploying Infrastructure with CloudFormation:** Automating the deployment of the application's infrastructure using AWS CloudFormation templates.
- **Monitoring and Managing Costs:** Implementing cost-effective strategies, such as using spot instances for non-critical workloads.

Conclusion

This chapter has provided an in-depth understanding of building scalable web applications on AWS. We explored multi-tier architectures, serverless designs, database optimization strategies, asynchronous processing, and monitoring practices. These concepts form the foundation for creating scalable and resilient web applications that can handle dynamic user demand and support business growth.

In the next chapter, we will delve into **"Microservices and Containerization"** to explore how microservices-based architectures and container technologies like ECS, EKS, and Docker enhance scalability, modularity, and resilience in cloud-based applications.

Chapter 3: Microservices and Containerization

Overview

Modern application architectures have evolved from traditional monolithic designs to more flexible and scalable approaches like microservices. By breaking down an application into smaller, independently deployable components, microservices allow for enhanced scalability, fault tolerance, and easier maintenance. In this chapter, we explore the principles of microservices architecture, the role of containerization, and how AWS services like ECS, EKS, and Fargate enable scalable microservices-based solutions.

1. Understanding Microservices Architecture

1.1 From Monolith to Microservices

Traditionally, applications were built as monolithic architectures, where all components—business logic, data access, and UI—were tightly coupled. This design led to challenges such as:

- **Difficulty in Scaling:** Monoliths often scale vertically, leading to limitations in handling large-scale workloads.

- **Complex Deployments:** Changes to a single component often required redeploying the entire application.
- **Tight Coupling:** Dependencies between components made updates and maintenance difficult.

Microservices architecture solves these problems by dividing an application into loosely coupled, independently deployable services, each responsible for a specific business capability. This approach offers several advantages:

- **Independent Scalability:** Each service can be scaled independently based on demand.
- **Flexible Technology Stack:** Each service can use a different technology stack or language best suited for its needs.
- **Fault Isolation:** Failures in one service do not impact the entire system, increasing overall reliability.

1.2 Characteristics of Microservices

Key characteristics of microservices include:

- **Single Responsibility Principle:** Each microservice is responsible for a specific business capability.
- **Decentralized Data Management:** Each service typically manages its database or data store to avoid tight coupling.
- **Automated Deployment:** Microservices can be independently developed, tested, and deployed using CI/CD pipelines.
- **API-Based Communication:** Microservices communicate with each other using lightweight APIs, usually over HTTP/REST, gRPC, or message queues.

1.3 Challenges in Implementing Microservices

While microservices architecture offers many benefits, it also presents several challenges:

- **Complexity in Orchestration:** Managing multiple services requires robust orchestration and monitoring tools.
- **Increased Latency:** Communication between services over the network can introduce latency.
- **Data Consistency:** Achieving data consistency across distributed services can be challenging.

2. Introduction to Containerization

2.1 The Role of Containers in Microservices

Containers are a lightweight virtualization technology that encapsulates an application and its dependencies into a single, isolated unit. They play a crucial role in microservices architecture by:

- **Ensuring Consistency Across Environments:** Containers package everything needed to run an application, ensuring that it behaves consistently across development, testing, and production environments.
- **Improving Resource Utilization:** Containers allow multiple applications to run on the same host without interfering with each other, leading to better resource utilization.
- **Simplifying Scalability:** Containers can be easily replicated and scaled across multiple hosts or clusters.

2.2 Docker: The Foundation of Containerization

Docker is the most popular containerization platform. Key features of Docker that support scalable microservices include:

- **Docker Images:** Lightweight, immutable snapshots of an application and its dependencies.
- **Docker Containers:** Isolated instances of Docker images that run applications.
- **Docker Compose:** A tool for defining and running multi-container applications.

- **Docker Swarm and Kubernetes:** Orchestration platforms that automate the deployment and management of containerized applications.

2.3 Orchestrating Containers with Kubernetes

Kubernetes (K8s) is a powerful open-source container orchestration platform that simplifies the management of containerized applications. Core components of Kubernetes include:

- **Pods:** The smallest deployable units in Kubernetes, containing one or more containers.
- **Deployments:** Automate the creation, scaling, and management of pods.
- **Services:** Provide a stable network endpoint to expose containers.
- **Ingress Controllers:** Manage external access to services using HTTP/HTTPS routing.

3. Building Microservices with AWS ECS, EKS, and Fargate

3.1 Amazon Elastic Container Service (ECS)

Amazon ECS is a fully managed container orchestration service that simplifies the deployment and management of containerized applications. Key features of ECS include:

- **Task Definitions:** Define the containers, CPU, memory, and networking settings for your services.
- **ECS Clusters:** Logical groups of EC2 instances or Fargate tasks where containers are deployed.
- **Service Discovery:** Automatically registers and deregisters containers with DNS.

3.2 Amazon Elastic Kubernetes Service (EKS)

Amazon EKS provides a managed Kubernetes experience, allowing you to run Kubernetes clusters without managing the underlying infrastructure. Key features of EKS include:

- **Managed Node Groups:** Automate the provisioning and scaling of EC2 instances for your Kubernetes clusters.
- **Integration with AWS Services:** EKS integrates seamlessly with AWS services like ALB, IAM, and CloudWatch.
- **Cluster Auto Scaling:** Automatically adjusts the size of your cluster based on resource requirements.

3.3 AWS Fargate for Serverless Containers

AWS Fargate is a serverless compute engine that runs containers without requiring you to manage servers. It works with both ECS and EKS, providing:

- **Simplified Scaling:** Automatically scales containers based on task requirements.
- **Reduced Management Overhead:** Abstracts infrastructure management, allowing you to focus on building applications.

4. Designing Scalable Microservices Architectures

4.1 Implementing Service Communication

Microservices communicate with each other using a variety of methods, including:

- **Synchronous Communication:** HTTP/REST or gRPC-based communication for real-time requests.
- **Asynchronous Communication:** Event-driven communication using message queues like AWS SQS or streaming services like AWS Kinesis.
- **Service Mesh:** Using tools like Istio or AWS App Mesh to manage complex communication between microservices.

4.2 Handling Data Persistence in Microservices

Data persistence in microservices can be challenging due to the need for independent databases. Strategies for managing data include:

- **Database per Service:** Each service manages its database to ensure loose coupling and independent scaling.
- **Event Sourcing:** Storing a sequence of events that represent changes in state, which allows for eventual consistency.
- **CQRS (Command Query Responsibility Segregation):** Separating read and write operations into different models to improve scalability.

4.3 Managing Distributed Transactions

Distributed transactions across multiple services require careful coordination. Techniques to handle distributed transactions include:

- **Two-Phase Commit (2PC):** A protocol to ensure atomic transactions, but with performance trade-offs.
- **Saga Pattern:** A distributed transaction pattern where each service performs a local transaction and publishes an event for the next service in the workflow.

5. Monitoring and Managing Microservices at Scale

5.1 Implementing Observability with AWS CloudWatch and X-Ray

Observability in microservices involves monitoring, logging, and tracing. Key components of observability include:

- **CloudWatch Metrics and Alarms:** Monitor CPU, memory, network traffic, and custom metrics.
- **Centralized Logging with CloudWatch Logs:** Aggregate logs from different services for better visibility.
- **AWS X-Ray:** Trace requests across distributed services to identify bottlenecks and latency issues.

5.2 Performance Optimization Techniques

Optimize the performance of microservices-based applications by:

- **Right-Sizing Containers:** Adjusting container resource limits to avoid over-provisioning or resource starvation.
- **Load Balancing and Traffic Shaping:** Using ALB and Route 53 to efficiently distribute traffic between services.
- **Horizontal Pod Autoscaling (HPA):** Automatically adjust the number of pods in Kubernetes based on real-time metrics.

6. Securing Microservices and Containers

6.1 Implementing Role-Based Access Control (RBAC)

RBAC is a security model that restricts system access based on roles. In a microservices architecture, RBAC is essential for managing:

- **User Permissions:** Defining who can access and modify services or resources.
- **Service-to-Service Communication:** Controlling which microservices can communicate with each other.

6.2 Using AWS IAM for Access Control

AWS Identity and Access Management (IAM) provides granular control over access to AWS resources. Key best practices include:

- **Creating Least-Privilege IAM Policies:** Grant the minimum required permissions to users and services.
- **Using IAM Roles for ECS and EKS:** Assign roles to containers to control access to other AWS services.

6.3 Securing Container Deployments with ECR and AWS Secrets Manager

To secure containerized applications, consider:

- **Storing Container Images in Amazon ECR:** Use ECR for secure and scalable image storage.

- **Managing Secrets with AWS Secrets Manager:** Store and retrieve database credentials, API keys, and other sensitive information securely.

7. Real-World Case Studies: Migrating a Monolith to Microservices on AWS

7.1 Overview of the Migration Process

This section provides a detailed case study of migrating a monolithic e-commerce application to a microservices architecture on AWS. The key objectives include improving scalability, reducing deployment time, and isolating failures.

7.2 Architectural Design and Key Decisions

Explain the architecture of the new microservices-based e-commerce platform, including:

- **Service Decomposition:** Identifying and breaking down core functionalities into separate microservices.
- **Container Orchestration with ECS:** Deploying microservices using ECS clusters and Fargate tasks.
- **Data Partitioning and Management:** Managing independent databases for each microservice and using DynamoDB for high-throughput operations.

7.3 Implementation and Best Practices

Detail the implementation process, including:

- **Automated Deployments with CodePipeline:** Setting up CI/CD pipelines for each microservice using AWS CodePipeline.
- **Monitoring and Observability:** Implementing CloudWatch dashboards and X-Ray tracing to monitor service health and performance.

Conclusion

In this chapter, we explored the principles of microservices architecture, the role of containerization, and how AWS services like ECS, EKS, and Fargate enable scalable solutions. We discussed service communication methods, data persistence strategies, and techniques for managing distributed transactions. By following the best practices and examples outlined in this chapter, you can build scalable, resilient, and secure microservices-based applications on AWS.

The next chapter will delve into **"Architecting for High Availability and Redundancy,"** focusing on multi-region deployments, cross-region replication, and fault-tolerant architecture design.

Chapter 4: Architecting for High Availability and Redundancy

Overview

I n cloud architecture, high availability (HA) and redundancy are crucial elements to ensure that applications are resilient, reliable, and accessible at all times. High availability focuses on minimizing downtime and service disruptions, while redundancy ensures that critical system components have backups in case of failures. This chapter explores the key principles of HA, best practices, and the AWS services that enable you to build highly available and redundant cloud solutions.

1. Principles of High Availability and Redundancy

1.1 Defining High Availability and Redundancy

High availability refers to the ability of a system to remain operational and accessible with minimal downtime, even in the event of hardware or software failures. The primary goal of HA is to ensure that services and applications are always accessible to end-users. Key attributes of high availability include:

- **Uptime and Reliability:** The percentage of time the system is available for use. A common target for high availability is 99.99% uptime or higher.

- **Fault Tolerance:** The ability of a system to continue operating correctly even when one or more of its components fail.
- **Disaster Recovery:** The process of recovering from catastrophic failures, such as data center outages or region-wide failures.

Redundancy, on the other hand, involves duplicating critical system components and functions to create backup systems that can take over if the primary components fail. Redundancy plays a key role in achieving HA and improving fault tolerance.

1.2 Importance of High Availability in Cloud Applications

The importance of high availability in cloud applications cannot be overstated, especially for mission-critical services like e-commerce platforms, financial systems, and healthcare applications. Key benefits include:

- **Improved User Experience:** Minimized downtime ensures that users can access services without disruptions.
- **Increased Business Continuity:** Redundant and highly available systems can continue to function even during partial failures.
- **Enhanced Reputation and Trust:** Businesses with reliable services build customer trust and loyalty.

2. Key Strategies for Architecting High Availability

2.1 Designing Multi-AZ and Multi-Region Architectures

One of the most effective strategies for achieving high availability is to distribute application components across multiple Availability Zones (AZs) or Regions. AWS provides several options to implement these architectures:

- **Multi-AZ Deployments:** Distributing instances and services across multiple Availability Zones within a single AWS Region. This helps mitigate the impact of data center failures.
- **Multi-Region Deployments:** Distributing instances and services across

multiple AWS Regions to ensure resilience against region-wide outages. Multi-Region architectures also improve latency by serving users from geographically closer locations.

2.2 Load Balancing and Traffic Distribution

Load balancing is critical for distributing incoming traffic across multiple instances or services. It helps prevent overloading a single instance and ensures that the failure of one instance does not impact the overall system. AWS provides several load balancing options:

- **Elastic Load Balancing (ELB):** Automatically distributes incoming application traffic across multiple EC2 instances or containers. AWS offers three types of load balancers:
- **Application Load Balancer (ALB):** Ideal for HTTP/HTTPS traffic with advanced routing capabilities.
- **Network Load Balancer (NLB):** Designed for ultra-low latency and high-throughput TCP traffic.
- **Gateway Load Balancer (GWLB):** Distributes traffic to virtual appliances like firewalls or security services.
- **Route 53 for DNS-Based Load Balancing:** AWS Route 53 allows you to implement DNS-based load balancing and global traffic routing using health checks and routing policies.

2.3 Implementing Data Replication and Backup

Data is the lifeblood of most applications, and ensuring its availability is a key aspect of high availability architecture. AWS offers several services and features to replicate and back up data:

- **RDS Multi-AZ Deployments:** Automatically replicate data to a standby instance in a different AZ, ensuring high availability for relational databases.
- **DynamoDB Global Tables:** Provide multi-region, fully replicated NoSQL tables that automatically synchronize data across multiple

Regions.

- **S3 Cross-Region Replication (CRR):** Replicates objects stored in Amazon S3 to another bucket in a different Region, ensuring high data availability and redundancy.

3. Best Practices for Achieving High Availability

3.1 Designing for Fault Tolerance

Fault tolerance involves designing systems that can continue to operate correctly in the event of failures. Key strategies include:

- **Using Auto Scaling:** Automatically adjust the number of EC2 instances or containers based on predefined thresholds to handle varying traffic loads.
- **Implementing Circuit Breakers:** In microservices architectures, use circuit breakers to detect service failures and prevent cascading failures by routing requests to fallback services or error handlers.
- **Decoupling Components:** Break down applications into loosely coupled components using services like Amazon SQS or SNS to minimize dependencies between components.

3.2 Monitoring and Alerting for High Availability

Proactive monitoring and alerting are essential for identifying issues before they impact users. AWS CloudWatch provides comprehensive monitoring capabilities, including:

- **CloudWatch Metrics and Dashboards:** Track key metrics like CPU utilization, latency, and error rates to identify potential problems.
- **CloudWatch Alarms:** Set up alarms that trigger notifications or automated actions when thresholds are breached.
- **AWS X-Ray:** Trace requests across distributed services to identify performance bottlenecks and latency issues.

3.3 Implementing Disaster Recovery Strategies

Disaster recovery (DR) is a crucial component of high availability. DR involves creating plans and strategies to recover from catastrophic failures, such as data center outages or security breaches. Key disaster recovery strategies include:

- **Pilot Light:** Maintain a minimal version of the application infrastructure that can be scaled up quickly in the event of a disaster.
- **Warm Standby:** Keep a scaled-down version of the production environment running in a different Region, ready to take over if the primary environment fails.
- **Multi-Region Active-Active:** Operate fully functional environments in multiple Regions simultaneously, providing seamless failover and low-latency access.

4. Implementing High Availability Using AWS Services

4.1 High Availability with Amazon EC2

EC2 forms the backbone of many AWS applications. To achieve high availability with EC2:

- **Multi-AZ Deployments:** Distribute EC2 instances across multiple Availability Zones within a Region.
- **Elastic IPs and Elastic Network Interfaces (ENIs):** Use Elastic IPs and ENIs to ensure that network configurations remain consistent during instance failures or migrations.
- **Auto Scaling Groups:** Create Auto Scaling Groups to automatically adjust the number of EC2 instances based on demand and maintain high availability.

4.2 High Availability with Amazon RDS and Aurora

Amazon RDS and Aurora offer several features for achieving high availability for relational databases:

- **Multi-AZ Deployments:** Enable Multi-AZ deployments to automatically replicate data to a standby instance in a different AZ.
- **Aurora Global Databases:** Allow you to replicate databases across multiple Regions, providing low-latency read access and disaster recovery capabilities.
- **Read Replicas:** Create read replicas to offload read-heavy workloads and improve performance without impacting the primary database.

4.3 High Availability with Amazon DynamoDB

DynamoDB provides several features for building highly available and scalable NoSQL databases:

- **Global Tables:** Replicate DynamoDB tables across multiple Regions for low-latency access and disaster recovery.
- **On-Demand and Provisioned Capacity Modes:** Automatically scale read and write capacity based on traffic patterns.
- **DynamoDB Streams:** Capture changes to DynamoDB tables and use AWS Lambda to react to those changes in real-time.

5. Architecting Multi-Region Solutions for Global Availability

5.1 Multi-Region Architectures and Benefits

Multi-Region architectures provide resilience against regional failures and improve user experience by serving requests from the nearest Region. Benefits include:

- **Improved Latency:** Serve users from geographically closer Regions, reducing latency.
- **Increased Resilience:** Minimize the impact of Region-wide outages by replicating critical components across multiple Regions.

5.2 Implementing Cross-Region Replication and Failover

Cross-Region replication and failover are critical components of multi-

Region architectures. AWS provides several services and features for implementing these capabilities:

- **Amazon RDS Global Databases:** Enable cross-Region replication for Amazon Aurora databases, providing low-latency read access and automated failover.
- **Route 53 Failover Routing:** Use Route 53 to automatically route traffic to healthy endpoints in a different Region in the event of a failure.
- **S3 Cross-Region Replication (CRR):** Automatically replicate S3 objects to another bucket in a different Region.

5.3 Managing Data Consistency Across Regions

Achieving data consistency across multiple Regions can be challenging, especially in distributed architectures. Strategies to manage data consistency include:

- **Eventual Consistency for Distributed Databases:** Accept some level of eventual consistency for applications that do not require strict consistency.
- **Using AWS Global Accelerator:** Provide low-latency access to static or dynamic content stored in multiple Regions.
- **DynamoDB Global Tables:** Provide strong consistency within Regions and eventual consistency across Regions, making them suitable for multi-Region applications.

6. Case Study: Building a Highly Available E-commerce Platform on AWS

6.1 Overview of the E-commerce Platform Requirements

This case study focuses on designing and implementing a highly available e-commerce platform using AWS. Key requirements include:

- **Handling traffic spikes during sales events.**
- **Ensuring minimal downtime during maintenance.**
- **Providing a seamless shopping experience for users.**

6.2 Architectural Design and Key Decisions

Explain the architecture of the e-commerce platform, including:

- **Multi-AZ and Multi-Region Deployments:** Distributing application components across multiple Availability Zones and Regions for redundancy and high availability.
- **Load Balancing:** Using an Application Load Balancer (ALB) to distribute incoming traffic evenly across EC2 instances and containers.

6.3 Implementation and Best Practices

Detail the implementation process, including:

- **Automated Deployments with CloudFormation:** Using AWS CloudFormation to automate the provisioning of infrastructure.
- **Monitoring and Alerts:** Implementing CloudWatch alarms and dashboards to monitor the health and performance of the application.

Conclusion

In this chapter, we explored the principles of high availability and redundancy, strategies for architecting highly available systems, and AWS services that enable high availability. We discussed best practices for designing fault-tolerant architectures and implementing multi-Region solutions for global availability. By following the concepts outlined in this chapter, you can build resilient and scalable applications on AWS that ensure continuous availability and performance.

The next chapter will focus on **"Data Security and Compliance in AWS,"** discussing strategies and services to protect your applications and data in the cloud.

Chapter 5: Data Security and Compliance in AWS

Overview

I n an era where data breaches and security threats are commonplace, protecting sensitive information and ensuring compliance with regulations have become paramount for businesses. As organizations increasingly migrate to the cloud, understanding how to secure data and applications in the AWS environment is critical. This chapter explores the principles of data security, key AWS services that enhance security, best practices for securing cloud applications, and the importance of compliance in cloud computing.

1. Understanding Data Security in the Cloud

1.1 Defining Data Security

Data security involves protecting digital information from unauthorized access, corruption, or theft. In the cloud context, it encompasses a range of practices and technologies designed to ensure the confidentiality, integrity, and availability of data. Key components of data security include:

- **Confidentiality:** Ensuring that only authorized users have access to sensitive information.
- **Integrity:** Protecting data from unauthorized modification or deletion.
- **Availability:** Ensuring that data and applications are accessible when needed.

1.2 The Shared Responsibility Model

AWS operates under a shared responsibility model, which delineates the responsibilities of AWS and its customers in maintaining security. This model consists of:

- **AWS Responsibility:** AWS manages security **of** the cloud, including the physical security of data centers, network infrastructure, and hardware. This also includes ensuring that the underlying services are secure.
- **Customer Responsibility:** Customers are responsible for security **in** the cloud, including managing access controls, data encryption, and configuring services securely.

Understanding this model is essential for implementing effective security measures in AWS.

2. Key AWS Security Services

2.1 Identity and Access Management (IAM)

AWS IAM is a cornerstone service for managing user access and permissions. It allows you to create and manage AWS users and groups and define permissions for those users. Key features include:

- **Fine-Grained Access Control:** IAM policies allow you to specify who can access which resources and what actions they can perform.
- **Multi-Factor Authentication (MFA):** Enhances security by requiring users to provide additional verification beyond just a password.
- **IAM Roles:** Enable you to delegate access to AWS resources without

sharing long-term credentials.

2.2 AWS Key Management Service (KMS)

AWS KMS is a fully managed service that makes it easy to create and control the encryption keys used to encrypt data. Key features include:

- **Centralized Key Management:** Allows you to manage encryption keys across AWS services and applications.
- **Integrated with AWS Services:** Many AWS services integrate with KMS for data encryption, including S3, EBS, and RDS.
- **Audit Logging:** KMS provides detailed logs of key usage through AWS CloudTrail.

2.3 AWS CloudTrail

AWS CloudTrail is a service that enables governance, compliance, and operational and risk auditing of your AWS account. Key features include:

- **Event Logging:** Automatically records account activity and API calls made on your account, providing visibility into user actions.
- **Integrations with AWS Services:** Works seamlessly with other AWS services to enhance security monitoring.
- **Data Integrity:** Ensures the integrity of logs by maintaining them in a secure manner.

2.4 Amazon GuardDuty

Amazon GuardDuty is a threat detection service that continuously monitors for malicious activity and unauthorized behavior. Key features include:

- **Intelligent Threat Detection:** Uses machine learning and threat intelligence to identify potential security threats.
- **Automated Alerts:** Sends alerts when potential security issues are detected, enabling rapid response.
- **Integration with AWS Security Hub:** Centralizes security findings

from various AWS services.

2.5 AWS Shield and AWS WAF

AWS Shield is a managed Distributed Denial of Service (DDoS) protection service, while AWS Web Application Firewall (WAF) helps protect applications from web exploits. Key features include:

- **AWS Shield:** Provides automatic protection against DDoS attacks, with advanced features available in Shield Advanced.
- **AWS WAF:** Allows you to create rules to filter out malicious traffic based on patterns, IP addresses, and request attributes.
- **Integration with ALB and CloudFront:** Both services can be easily integrated with AWS Shield and WAF for enhanced protection.

3. Best Practices for Securing AWS Environments

3.1 Implementing the Principle of Least Privilege

The principle of least privilege ensures that users have only the permissions necessary to perform their job functions. Best practices include:

- **Role-Based Access Control (RBAC):** Assign permissions based on roles rather than individual users to simplify management.
- **Regularly Review IAM Policies:** Conduct audits of IAM policies to ensure they adhere to the principle of least privilege.
- **Temporary Credentials:** Use temporary security credentials to limit the duration of access.

3.2 Data Encryption Strategies

Encrypting data is vital for protecting sensitive information both at rest and in transit. Strategies include:

- **Encrypting Data at Rest:** Use AWS KMS to manage encryption keys for data stored in S3, EBS, RDS, and other services.

- **Encrypting Data in Transit:** Implement TLS/SSL for data transmitted between applications and AWS services to prevent interception.
- **Using Amazon S3 Bucket Policies:** Enforce encryption on S3 buckets to ensure that all objects are encrypted upon upload.

3.3 Regular Security Audits and Assessments

Conducting regular security audits and assessments helps identify vulnerabilities and improve security posture. Best practices include:

- **AWS Config:** Use AWS Config to monitor and assess the compliance of AWS resources against security best practices.
- **Penetration Testing:** Conduct penetration testing to identify potential security weaknesses and vulnerabilities.
- **Third-Party Security Assessments:** Engage third-party security experts to evaluate your AWS architecture for vulnerabilities.

4. Compliance in the Cloud

4.1 Understanding Cloud Compliance

Compliance in the cloud involves adhering to legal, regulatory, and industry standards regarding data protection and security. Organizations must ensure that their cloud practices align with applicable regulations, such as:

- **General Data Protection Regulation (GDPR):** EU regulation that governs data protection and privacy.
- **Health Insurance Portability and Accountability Act (HIPAA):** U.S. regulation that mandates data privacy and security provisions for safeguarding medical information.
- **Payment Card Industry Data Security Standard (PCI DSS):** A set of security standards for organizations that handle credit card information.

4.2 AWS Compliance Programs

AWS provides a wide range of compliance certifications and attestations to help customers meet regulatory requirements. Key compliance programs include:

- **ISO Certifications:** AWS is ISO 27001 certified, demonstrating its commitment to information security management.
- **SOC Reports:** AWS regularly undergoes independent audits to assess controls and processes against SOC 1, SOC 2, and SOC 3 standards.
- **HIPAA Compliance:** AWS offers services compliant with HIPAA, enabling healthcare organizations to store and process sensitive medical data securely.

4.3 Implementing Compliance Controls in AWS

To implement compliance controls in AWS, organizations should:

- **Use AWS Artifact:** A self-service portal that provides on-demand access to AWS compliance documentation and reports.
- **Enable CloudTrail for Audit Trails:** Use AWS CloudTrail to maintain audit logs of all API calls and activities in the AWS account.
- **Leverage AWS Config Rules:** Create AWS Config rules to ensure resources comply with security and regulatory standards.

5. Incident Response and Recovery

5.1 Developing an Incident Response Plan

An incident response plan outlines procedures for detecting, responding to, and recovering from security incidents. Key components include:

- **Incident Detection:** Implement monitoring tools (e.g., AWS CloudWatch, GuardDuty) to detect potential security incidents.
- **Incident Classification:** Establish criteria for classifying incidents based on severity and impact.
- **Response Procedures:** Define roles and responsibilities for the incident response team and outline steps for containing and mitigating incidents.

5.2 Utilizing AWS Services for Incident Response

AWS provides several services to enhance incident response capabilities:

- **AWS Lambda for Automation:** Use Lambda functions to automate responses to security incidents, such as isolating compromised resources or adjusting security group settings.
- **AWS Systems Manager:** Use Systems Manager for managing and automating operational tasks during incidents.
- **Amazon SNS for Notifications:** Set up notifications through Amazon SNS to alert stakeholders about incidents in real-time.

6. Case Study: Securing a Financial Application on AWS

6.1 Overview of the Financial Application Requirements

This case study examines the security measures implemented to protect a financial application deployed on AWS. Key requirements include:

- **Compliance with PCI DSS regulations.**
- **Protection of sensitive user data, such as credit card information.**
- **Ensuring high availability and reliability.**

6.2 Architectural Design and Key Security Measures

Explain the security architecture of the financial application, including:

- **Using VPCs for Network Isolation:** The application was deployed in a dedicated VPC, ensuring network isolation and enhanced security.
- **Implementing IAM Roles and Policies:** Fine-grained access control was achieved using IAM roles and policies to restrict access to sensitive resources.
- **Data Encryption:** All sensitive data at rest and in transit was encrypted using AWS KMS and TLS/SSL.

6.3 Implementation and Best Practices

Detail the implementation process, including:

- **Regular Security Audits:** Conducted regular security audits and vulnerability assessments to ensure compliance with PCI DSS.
- **Monitoring and Incident Response:** Utilized CloudWatch and Guard-Duty for continuous monitoring and alerting of potential security incidents.

Conclusion

In this chapter, we explored the essential aspects of data security and compliance in AWS. We covered key AWS security services, best practices for securing cloud environments, compliance considerations, and incident response strategies. Understanding and implementing these security measures is critical for building resilient applications and protecting sensitive data in the cloud.

In the next chapter, we will focus on **"Cost Management and Optimization in AWS,"** discussing strategies and tools to monitor and optimize AWS costs while maintaining performance and scalability.

Chapter 6: Cost Management and Optimization in AWS

Overview

As organizations transition to the cloud, understanding and managing costs effectively becomes a critical aspect of cloud strategy. AWS offers a wide range of services that provide flexibility and scalability, but these benefits can also lead to unpredictable costs if not managed properly. This chapter will explore the principles of cost management in AWS, the tools available for monitoring and optimizing costs, and best practices for ensuring that cloud spending aligns with business goals.

1. Understanding Cost Management in AWS

1.1 Defining Cost Management

Cost management involves planning and controlling the budget of a business, which in the cloud context includes tracking and optimizing cloud expenditures. Key components include:

- **Cost Tracking:** Monitoring the costs associated with AWS services and understanding where money is being spent.

- **Budgeting:** Establishing a financial plan that outlines expected costs and resource usage.
- **Forecasting:** Predicting future costs based on current usage patterns and business growth.

1.2 The Importance of Cost Management in the Cloud

Effective cost management in AWS is crucial for several reasons:

- **Avoiding Overspending:** Without proper monitoring, organizations can incur unexpected charges, leading to budget overruns.
- **Resource Optimization:** Understanding usage patterns helps organizations make informed decisions about resource allocation and scaling.
- **Strategic Planning:** Cost management insights can inform strategic decisions about cloud investments, migration, and expansion.

2. AWS Pricing Models

2.1 Pay-as-You-Go Pricing

AWS operates on a pay-as-you-go pricing model, meaning that customers only pay for the resources they use. Key benefits include:

- **No Upfront Costs:** Organizations do not need to invest in hardware or infrastructure upfront.
- **Scalability:** Costs scale with usage, allowing organizations to adapt to changing demands without incurring unnecessary expenses.

2.2 Reserved Instances and Savings Plans

To provide more cost predictability, AWS offers Reserved Instances (RIs) and Savings Plans, which allow customers to commit to using AWS services for a specific term in exchange for lower rates.

- **Reserved Instances:** Offer significant discounts (up to 75%) for committing to use EC2 instances for a one or three-year term. There are

Standard and Convertible RIs, with the latter allowing changes to the instance type.

- **Savings Plans:** Flexible pricing model that provides savings on usage across various services (like EC2, Fargate, and Lambda) in exchange for a commitment to a specific amount of usage.

2.3 Spot Instances

AWS Spot Instances allow customers to bid on unused EC2 capacity, often at substantial discounts compared to On-Demand pricing. This model is ideal for:

- **Flexible Workloads:** Applications that can tolerate interruptions, such as batch processing or data analysis tasks.
- **Cost-Conscious Operations:** Organizations looking to optimize costs without compromising on the required compute resources.

3. Tools for Cost Monitoring and Management

3.1 AWS Cost Explorer

AWS Cost Explorer is a powerful tool that enables users to visualize and analyze their AWS spending over time. Key features include:

- **Cost and Usage Reports:** Detailed reports that provide insights into spending patterns and resource usage.
- **Forecasting Capabilities:** Ability to forecast future costs based on historical usage data.
- **Filtering and Grouping:** Users can filter and group data by service, tags, and accounts to gain deeper insights.

3.2 AWS Budgets

AWS Budgets allows organizations to set custom cost and usage budgets that track their spending against defined thresholds. Key functionalities include:

- **Alerts and Notifications:** Users can receive alerts when costs exceed budget thresholds or are forecasted to exceed budgets.
- **Multiple Budget Types:** Organizations can create budgets for costs, usage, reservations, or savings plans.

3.3 AWS Cost and Usage Reports

AWS Cost and Usage Reports provide detailed information about resource usage and costs, enabling organizations to perform in-depth analysis. Key features include:

- **CSV and Parquet Formats:** Reports can be generated in different formats for easier analysis in data processing tools.
- **Integration with BI Tools:** Users can integrate these reports with business intelligence tools for enhanced reporting and visualization.

4. Best Practices for Cost Optimization in AWS

4.1 Rightsizing Resources

Rightsizing involves selecting the optimal resource sizes to meet application requirements without over-provisioning. Best practices include:

- **Monitoring Usage Metrics:** Regularly review CloudWatch metrics to analyze resource utilization patterns and adjust instance sizes accordingly.
- **Using AWS Trusted Advisor:** A service that provides real-time guidance to help provision your resources following AWS best practices, including cost optimization recommendations.

4.2 Implementing Auto Scaling

Auto Scaling enables organizations to automatically adjust the number of running instances based on demand, helping to optimize costs. Key strategies include:

- **Configuring Scaling Policies:** Set up policies that trigger scaling actions based on CloudWatch metrics, such as CPU utilization or network traffic.
- **Using Scheduled Scaling:** Automatically adjust the capacity of your application during predictable traffic patterns (e.g., scaling up during business hours).

4.3 Leveraging S3 Storage Classes

Amazon S3 offers various storage classes to help organizations optimize costs based on access patterns. Best practices include:

- **Lifecycle Policies:** Automatically transition objects to lower-cost storage classes, such as S3 Glacier, based on data access patterns.
- **Intelligent-Tiering:** Use the S3 Intelligent-Tiering storage class to automatically move data between frequent and infrequent access tiers based on changing access patterns.

4.4 Optimizing Data Transfer Costs

Data transfer costs can significantly impact overall AWS spending. Strategies to optimize data transfer costs include:

- **Using CloudFront:** Employ Amazon CloudFront, a content delivery network (CDN), to cache and deliver content closer to users, reducing data transfer costs from the origin server.
- **Minimizing Cross-Region Data Transfers:** Avoid unnecessary data transfers across AWS Regions by localizing services and data wherever possible.

5. Analyzing and Forecasting Costs

5.1 Cost Analysis Techniques

To effectively manage costs, organizations should employ various analysis techniques:

- **Tagging Resources:** Implement a robust tagging strategy to categorize resources by projects, departments, or environments. This enables more accurate cost allocation and analysis.
- **Comparative Analysis:** Regularly compare costs against budget forecasts and previous periods to identify trends and variances.

5.2 Cost Forecasting Methods

Accurate cost forecasting is essential for budget planning and resource allocation. Techniques include:

- **Utilizing AWS Cost Explorer Forecasting:** Leverage AWS Cost Explorer's forecasting capabilities to predict future spending based on historical data.
- **Implementing Machine Learning Models:** Consider using machine learning algorithms to analyze usage patterns and predict future costs based on historical trends.

6. Cost Governance and Accountability

6.1 Establishing Cost Governance Frameworks

A strong governance framework ensures that cloud spending aligns with organizational goals. Key components include:

- **Defining Roles and Responsibilities:** Assign accountability for cloud spending at various organizational levels (e.g., departmental budgets, project leads).
- **Implementing Policies and Guidelines:** Establish clear guidelines for resource provisioning, usage, and cost management practices.

6.2 Promoting Cost Awareness Across Teams

Fostering a culture of cost awareness can help optimize cloud spending across the organization. Strategies include:

- **Training and Workshops:** Conduct regular training sessions to educate teams about cost management best practices and tools.
- **Regular Reporting:** Provide visibility into cloud spending through regular reports and dashboards to encourage accountability.

7. Real-World Case Study: Cost Optimization for a SaaS Application

7.1 Overview of the SaaS Application

This case study examines a Software as a Service (SaaS) application that successfully optimized its AWS costs while maintaining performance and scalability. Key objectives included:

- **Reducing overall cloud expenditure by 30%.**
- **Improving resource utilization without impacting user experience.**

7.2 Architectural Overview and Initial Challenges

Discuss the initial architecture of the application, highlighting areas of inefficiency and cost overspending.

- **Over-Provisioned Resources:** Initial deployment had EC2 instances with excess capacity that led to unnecessary costs.
- **Inefficient Data Storage:** Data was primarily stored in standard S3 storage class, resulting in higher costs for infrequently accessed data.

7.3 Cost Optimization Strategies Implemented

Detail the cost optimization strategies employed, including:

- **Rightsizing and Auto Scaling:** Conducted a comprehensive review of resource utilization, implementing rightsizing and auto scaling for EC2 instances.
- **Implementing S3 Lifecycle Policies:** Transitioned infrequently accessed data to S3 Glacier, reducing storage costs.
- **Regular Cost Monitoring:** Established a cost monitoring process

using AWS Budgets and Cost Explorer to track spending and identify anomalies.

7.4 Results and Lessons Learned

Summarize the outcomes of the cost optimization initiatives, highlighting:

- **Cost Reduction:** Achieved a 30% reduction in overall AWS spending while maintaining performance.
- **Improved Resource Utilization:** Enhanced resource efficiency and responsiveness to changing traffic patterns.

Conclusion

In this chapter, we explored the principles of cost management and optimization in AWS. We covered AWS pricing models, tools for monitoring costs, best practices for optimizing spending, and real-world case studies that illustrate effective cost management strategies. Understanding and implementing these concepts are essential for organizations to maximize the value of their AWS investments while maintaining control over cloud spending.

In the next chapter, we will delve into **"Architecting for High Availability and Redundancy,"** focusing on strategies and AWS services that enhance system resilience and reliability.

Chapter 7: Monitoring and Logging in AWS

Overview

Effective monitoring and logging are essential for maintaining the health, performance, and security of applications running in the AWS cloud. They enable organizations to detect and respond to issues promptly, ensure compliance with regulations, and provide insights into system performance. This chapter explores the various AWS services and best practices for monitoring applications and logging activities, ensuring that organizations can achieve operational excellence in the cloud.

1. The Importance of Monitoring and Logging

1.1 Defining Monitoring and Logging

- **Monitoring:** The process of collecting, analyzing, and using performance data to ensure that systems are operating as expected. It includes tracking metrics related to system performance, availability, and resource usage.
- **Logging:** The act of recording events and activities within a system. Logs

provide detailed information about operations, errors, and user actions, which can be crucial for troubleshooting and forensic analysis.

1.2 Why Monitoring and Logging Matter

- **Proactive Issue Detection:** Monitoring helps identify issues before they escalate into serious problems, allowing for proactive remediation.
- **Performance Optimization:** Analyzing performance metrics can lead to insights that drive optimization efforts, improving application efficiency.
- **Compliance and Auditing:** Logging is essential for meeting compliance requirements and for conducting audits of access and usage patterns.
- **Enhanced Security:** Monitoring can help detect security incidents and anomalies, while logging provides valuable information for incident investigation.

2. Key AWS Monitoring Services

2.1 Amazon CloudWatch

Amazon CloudWatch is a comprehensive monitoring and management service for AWS resources and applications. Key features include:

- **Metrics Collection:** CloudWatch automatically collects and tracks metrics for AWS services, such as EC2 instance CPU utilization, RDS database connections, and S3 bucket requests.
- **Custom Metrics:** Users can define custom metrics for specific applications or business needs.
- **Alarms:** Set up alarms to trigger notifications or automated actions based on specified thresholds.

2.1.1 Setting Up CloudWatch Metrics and Alarms

- **Default Metrics:** Each AWS service provides a set of default metrics

that can be monitored out of the box.
- **Creating Alarms:** Step-by-step guidance on how to create CloudWatch alarms to notify teams when metrics exceed defined thresholds.

2.2 AWS CloudTrail

AWS CloudTrail is a service that enables governance, compliance, and operational auditing of your AWS account. It records API calls made on your account and provides event history. Key features include:

- **Event Logging:** Captures detailed information about API calls, including who made the call, what actions were taken, and from which IP address.
- **Integration with CloudWatch Logs:** CloudTrail logs can be sent to CloudWatch Logs for further analysis and monitoring.

2.2.1 Enabling CloudTrail and Analyzing Logs

- **Setting Up CloudTrail:** Instructions for enabling CloudTrail and configuring it to log events for all regions or specific services.
- **Analyzing CloudTrail Logs:** Techniques for querying and analyzing logs to monitor account activity and detect unauthorized access.

2.3 AWS Config

AWS Config is a service that enables you to assess, audit, and evaluate the configurations of your AWS resources. It provides:

- **Configuration Monitoring:** Tracks changes to AWS resources and their configurations over time.
- **Compliance Checking:** AWS Config can automatically check resource configurations against defined compliance policies.

2.3.1 Using AWS Config Rules

- **Creating Config Rules:** How to create and manage AWS Config rules to ensure compliance with best practices and security policies.

- **Remediation Actions:** Automating remediation actions when resources deviate from compliance standards.

3. AWS Logging Services

3.1 Amazon S3 for Log Storage

Amazon S3 is an ideal solution for storing log files generated by applications and AWS services. Key features include:

- **Durability and Availability:** S3 offers high durability and availability for stored logs.
- **Lifecycle Policies:** Automatically transition logs to cheaper storage classes, like S3 Glacier, after a defined period.

3.1.1 Best Practices for Storing Logs in S3

- **Organizing Log Data:** Techniques for organizing log data in S3 using prefixes and folders for easier retrieval.
- **Setting Up S3 Lifecycle Policies:** Step-by-step instructions on configuring lifecycle policies to manage log storage costs.

3.2 Amazon Elasticsearch Service (OpenSearch Service)

Amazon OpenSearch Service (formerly Elasticsearch) allows you to analyze and visualize log data in real-time. Key features include:

- **Search and Query Capabilities:** Supports complex searches and queries to extract insights from log data.
- **Integration with Kibana:** Use Kibana to create visualizations and dashboards for log data analysis.

3.2.1 Setting Up OpenSearch for Log Analysis

- **Indexing Logs:** Instructions for indexing logs stored in S3 or generated by applications into OpenSearch.
- **Creating Visualizations:** How to use Kibana to create meaningful visualizations from your log data.

4. Best Practices for Monitoring and Logging

4.1 Establishing a Monitoring Strategy

A well-defined monitoring strategy is essential for effective monitoring and logging. Considerations include:

- **Defining Key Performance Indicators (KPIs):** Identify the critical metrics that reflect the health and performance of your applications.
- **Implementing Dashboards:** Use CloudWatch Dashboards or OpenSearch Dashboards to provide a unified view of performance metrics and logs.

4.2 Log Management Best Practices

To effectively manage logs, follow these best practices:

- **Centralized Logging:** Aggregate logs from various sources into a centralized location (e.g., S3 or OpenSearch) for easier access and analysis.
- **Log Retention Policies:** Define clear retention policies based on compliance and operational needs.
- **Regular Log Analysis:** Conduct regular analysis of log data to identify trends, anomalies, and potential issues.

4.3 Security Considerations in Monitoring and Logging

Security is a critical aspect of monitoring and logging. Best practices include:

- **Access Controls:** Implement strict access controls to logging services and data to prevent unauthorized access.

- **Encryption:** Use encryption to protect sensitive log data at rest and in transit.
- **Audit Logging:** Ensure that security-related events are logged and monitored for compliance and forensic analysis.

5. Advanced Monitoring Techniques

5.1 Implementing Application Performance Monitoring (APM)

APM tools provide deeper insights into application performance and user experience. While AWS offers basic monitoring, integrating third-party APM tools can provide additional visibility. Key APM features include:

- **Transaction Tracing:** Monitor transactions across distributed systems to identify bottlenecks and latency issues.
- **User Experience Monitoring:** Track real user interactions to measure performance from the user's perspective.

5.1.1 Integrating APM Tools with AWS

- **Popular APM Tools:** Overview of popular APM solutions (e.g., New Relic, Dynatrace) and how they integrate with AWS services.
- **Configuring APM Agents:** Instructions for deploying APM agents in AWS environments for performance monitoring.

5.2 Implementing Serverless Monitoring

With the rise of serverless architectures, monitoring serverless applications is essential. AWS provides specific tools for this:

- **AWS Lambda Monitoring:** Use CloudWatch metrics to monitor Lambda functions, including invocation counts, errors, and duration.
- **AWS X-Ray for Distributed Tracing:** Use X-Ray to trace requests through serverless applications, providing insights into performance and issues.

6. Cost Management in Monitoring and Logging

6.1 Understanding Cost Implications
Monitoring and logging can incur significant costs if not managed properly. Considerations include:

- **Data Storage Costs:** Analyze costs associated with storing logs in S3, OpenSearch, or CloudWatch Logs.
- **Monitoring Service Costs:** Evaluate costs for AWS services like CloudWatch and X-Ray based on usage metrics.

6.2 Optimizing Monitoring and Logging Costs
To manage costs effectively, organizations should:

- **Implement Cost Controls:** Use AWS Budgets and Cost Explorer to track and control spending on monitoring and logging services.
- **Review Retention Policies:** Regularly review log retention policies to avoid unnecessary data storage costs.

7. Real-World Case Study: Monitoring a Web Application on AWS

7.1 Overview of the Web Application
This case study examines a web application deployed on AWS and the monitoring strategies implemented to ensure optimal performance and reliability. Key requirements include:

- **Real-time monitoring of application performance.**
- **Proactive identification of issues before they impact users.**

7.2 Architectural Overview and Initial Challenges
Discuss the initial architecture of the application, highlighting challenges faced in monitoring:

- **Lack of Visibility:** Initial deployment did not have effective monitoring in place, leading to delayed issue detection.
- **Siloed Data Sources:** Logs were stored in multiple locations, making analysis cumbersome.

7.3 Monitoring Strategy Implemented

Detail the monitoring strategy employed, including:

- **CloudWatch Integration:** Configured CloudWatch to monitor key metrics, set up alarms, and visualize data through dashboards.
- **Centralized Logging with S3:** Implemented centralized logging by storing application logs in S3 and integrating with OpenSearch for analysis.

7.4 Results and Lessons Learned

Summarize the outcomes of the monitoring implementation, highlighting:

- **Improved Incident Response:** Enhanced visibility led to faster identification and resolution of issues.
- **Optimized Performance:** Regular monitoring enabled performance tuning and resource optimization.

Conclusion

In this chapter, we explored the critical aspects of monitoring and logging in AWS. We covered key AWS services for monitoring and logging, best practices for effective monitoring strategies, advanced monitoring techniques, and real-world case studies. Implementing a robust monitoring and logging framework is essential for ensuring the reliability, performance, and security of applications running in the AWS cloud.

In the next chapter, we will focus on **"Disaster Recovery and Business Continuity,"** discussing strategies for ensuring operational resilience in the face of unexpected events.

Chapter 8: Disaster Recovery and Business Continuity in AWS

Overview

I n today's fast-paced digital landscape, businesses face numerous risks that could disrupt their operations, ranging from natural disasters to cyber-attacks. Therefore, developing robust disaster recovery (DR) and business continuity (BC) plans is essential for maintaining service availability and minimizing downtime. This chapter explores the concepts of disaster recovery and business continuity, the strategies to implement them effectively using AWS services, and best practices to ensure resilience in cloud architectures.

1. Understanding Disaster Recovery and Business Continuity

1.1 Defining Disaster Recovery

Disaster recovery refers to the strategies and processes that organizations implement to recover IT systems and operations after a disruptive event. Key aspects include:

- **Recovery Time Objective (RTO):** The maximum acceptable time that a system can be down after a disaster before operations can resume.

- **Recovery Point Objective (RPO):** The maximum acceptable amount of data loss measured in time; it indicates how far back in time the data must be restored.

1.2 Defining Business Continuity

Business continuity encompasses the plans and processes designed to ensure that critical business functions continue during and after a disaster. This includes:

- **Continuity of Operations:** Ensuring that essential services remain available, even during disruptions.
- **Crisis Management:** Coordinating responses to incidents to mitigate their impact and recover swiftly.

2. The Importance of Disaster Recovery and Business Continuity

2.1 Mitigating Risks

Disaster recovery and business continuity plans help organizations mitigate the risks associated with unexpected events, ensuring that they can recover quickly and maintain operations.

2.2 Protecting Brand Reputation

Minimizing downtime and maintaining service availability enhances customer trust and loyalty, protecting the organization's brand reputation.

2.3 Compliance and Regulatory Requirements

Many industries have regulatory requirements mandating disaster recovery and business continuity plans. Failing to comply can result in fines and legal repercussions.

3. AWS Disaster Recovery Strategies

3.1 AWS Regions and Availability Zones

AWS operates in multiple geographic regions and Availability Zones (AZs), providing the foundation for implementing disaster recovery strategies. Key considerations include:

- **Multi-AZ Deployments:** Deploying resources across multiple AZs within a single region enhances availability and resilience.
- **Multi-Region Deployments:** Distributing applications across multiple AWS regions provides additional redundancy and disaster recovery capabilities.

3.2 Backup and Restore Strategy

The backup and restore strategy is one of the simplest DR approaches. It involves regularly backing up data and restoring it when needed. AWS services that facilitate this include:

- **Amazon S3:** Use S3 for storing backups, leveraging its durability and availability features.
- **AWS Backup:** A fully managed backup service that simplifies the process of backing up AWS resources.

3.2.1 Implementing Backup Solutions

- **Regular Backup Schedules:** Establish a regular schedule for backing up critical data and applications.
- **Lifecycle Policies:** Use S3 lifecycle policies to manage backup data retention and cost effectively.

3.3 Pilot Light Strategy

The pilot light strategy involves maintaining a minimal version of an environment that can be scaled up in the event of a disaster. Key features include:

- **Critical Components:** Keeping only the essential components running, such as a database, to minimize costs.
- **Quick Recovery:** During a disaster, the environment can be quickly scaled to full capacity.

3.4 Warm Standby Strategy

The warm standby strategy involves maintaining a scaled-down version of a fully functional environment that can quickly be scaled up during a disaster. Key elements include:

- **Cost-Effective Maintenance:** Running a smaller version of the production environment reduces costs while ensuring readiness.
- **Rapid Recovery Time:** Because the environment is already operational, RTO is significantly reduced.

3.5 Multi-Site Strategy

The multi-site strategy involves maintaining two fully operational environments in different regions. Key benefits include:

- **High Availability:** Both environments are active and can handle production traffic.
- **Minimal RTO and RPO:** With both sites functioning, recovery time and data loss are minimized.

4. Implementing Business Continuity Plans

4.1 Developing a Business Continuity Plan

A business continuity plan outlines procedures to follow in the event of a disruption. Key components include:

- **Business Impact Analysis (BIA):** Identify critical business functions and the potential impact of disruptions.

- **Risk Assessment:** Evaluate risks and vulnerabilities to prioritize recovery efforts.

4.2 Roles and Responsibilities

Clearly define roles and responsibilities within the organization for managing and executing the business continuity plan. This includes:

- **Incident Response Team:** A designated team responsible for managing responses to incidents.
- **Communication Plans:** Establishing communication protocols for internal and external stakeholders during a disaster.

5. AWS Services for Disaster Recovery and Business Continuity

5.1 AWS Elastic Beanstalk

AWS Elastic Beanstalk is a Platform as a Service (PaaS) that simplifies deploying and managing applications. Key features include:

- **Environment Management:** Automatically handles provisioning, load balancing, and scaling of applications.
- **Integrated Monitoring:** Uses CloudWatch for monitoring application health and performance.

5.1.1 Implementing Disaster Recovery with Elastic Beanstalk

- **Environment Cloning:** Clone environments in different regions for quick deployment during a disaster.
- **Rolling Updates:** Use rolling updates to minimize downtime during application deployments.

5.2 Amazon RDS and Aurora

Amazon RDS and Aurora provide built-in features for disaster recovery:

- **Multi-AZ Deployments:** Automatically replicate databases to standby instances in different AZs for failover.
- **Read Replicas:** Use read replicas in different regions for cross-region disaster recovery.

5.2.1 Configuring RDS for High Availability

- **Creating Multi-AZ Deployments:** Step-by-step instructions for setting up Multi-AZ deployments for Amazon RDS.
- **Using Aurora Global Database:** Configure Aurora Global Database for low-latency cross-region disaster recovery.

5.3 AWS CloudFormation

AWS CloudFormation allows you to define your infrastructure as code. Key benefits include:

- **Infrastructure Automation:** Automate the deployment of resources in different regions for disaster recovery.
- **Version Control:** Use version-controlled templates to track changes and rollback if necessary.

5.3.1 Implementing CloudFormation for Disaster Recovery

- **Creating Stack Sets:** Use AWS CloudFormation StackSets to deploy resources across multiple accounts and regions simultaneously.
- **Automation with Lambda:** Integrate AWS Lambda functions for automated recovery processes triggered by CloudFormation events.

5.4 AWS Route 53

Amazon Route 53 is a scalable DNS web service that helps manage traffic routing and provides failover capabilities. Key features include:

- **Health Checks and DNS Failover:** Automatically reroute traffic to healthy endpoints in the event of a failure.

- **Geolocation Routing:** Serve users from the nearest region to reduce latency and improve performance.

5.4.1 Setting Up Route 53 for High Availability

- **Configuring Health Checks:** Instructions for setting up health checks for resources.
- **Implementing DNS Failover:** Step-by-step guidance on configuring DNS failover for disaster recovery.

6. Testing and Maintaining Disaster Recovery Plans

6.1 Importance of Testing DR Plans

Regularly testing disaster recovery plans is crucial for ensuring their effectiveness. Key reasons include:

- **Identifying Gaps:** Testing helps identify gaps and weaknesses in the DR plan.
- **Training Teams:** Regular drills ensure that teams are familiar with their roles and responsibilities during a disaster.

6.2 Types of Testing Approaches

Different testing approaches can be implemented to evaluate the effectiveness of DR plans:

- **Tabletop Exercises:** Conduct discussions to simulate a disaster scenario and assess response plans.
- **Simulation Testing:** Execute a simulated disaster to test the recovery process and team response.
- **Full Interruption Testing:** Involves shutting down systems to evaluate the full recovery process (should be conducted cautiously).

6.3 Continuous Improvement

Disaster recovery plans should be living documents that evolve with the organization. Best practices include:

- **Regular Reviews:** Schedule regular reviews of the DR plan to incorporate changes in technology, processes, or organizational structure.
- **Feedback Loop:** Establish a feedback mechanism to gather insights from tests and real incidents to improve the DR plan continuously.

7. Real-World Case Study: Disaster Recovery Planning for a Financial Institution

7.1 Overview of the Financial Institution

This case study examines how a financial institution implemented a comprehensive disaster recovery plan using AWS. Key objectives included:

- **Meeting stringent regulatory compliance requirements.**
- **Ensuring continuous access to financial services for customers.**

7.2 Architectural Overview and Initial Challenges

Discuss the initial architecture of the institution's applications, highlighting challenges faced in DR planning:

- **Legacy Systems:** Initial reliance on legacy systems with limited DR capabilities.
- **Regulatory Pressure:** Strict compliance requirements necessitating robust disaster recovery solutions.

7.3 Implementing the Disaster Recovery Plan

Detail the disaster recovery plan implemented, including:

- **AWS Services Utilized:** Using RDS Multi-AZ deployments, Route 53 for DNS failover, and S3 for backup.

- **Testing and Training:** Conducting regular DR drills to ensure preparedness.

7.4 Results and Lessons Learned

Summarize the outcomes of the disaster recovery implementation, highlighting:

- **Improved Compliance:** Successfully met regulatory compliance requirements with a robust DR plan.
- **Increased Confidence:** Enhanced confidence in service availability among stakeholders and customers.

Conclusion

In this chapter, we explored the critical aspects of disaster recovery and business continuity in AWS. We covered the importance of DR and BC, AWS strategies and services to implement these practices, and best practices for testing and maintaining DR plans. Understanding and implementing these concepts are essential for organizations to ensure resilience and minimize the impact of unexpected disruptions in the cloud.

In the next chapter, we will focus on **"Networking and Security in AWS,"** discussing strategies for securing cloud networks and ensuring data protection in transit and at rest.

Chapter 9: Networking and Security in AWS

Overview

Networking and security are critical components of cloud architecture in AWS. As organizations migrate to the cloud, ensuring the security of data and applications while maintaining efficient network performance becomes paramount. This chapter explores the principles of networking in AWS, key security measures, AWS services for secure networking, and best practices to protect cloud resources effectively.

1. Understanding Networking in AWS

1.1 Overview of AWS Networking Concepts

AWS provides a robust set of networking services and capabilities that facilitate secure and scalable connectivity between resources. Key concepts include:

- **Virtual Private Cloud (VPC):** A logically isolated network environment where users can define and control their virtual network.
- **Subnets:** Segments of a VPC that allow for organization and security of

resources.

- **Route Tables:** Determine how traffic is directed within a VPC and between subnets.

1.2 The Role of VPC in AWS Networking

A Virtual Private Cloud (VPC) is the foundation for networking in AWS. It enables users to create a private, isolated network within the AWS cloud. Key features include:

- **Subnet Configuration:** Users can create public and private subnets to control access to resources.
- **Internet Gateway:** Allows communication between resources in a VPC and the internet.
- **NAT Gateway:** Enables instances in a private subnet to initiate outbound traffic to the internet while preventing inbound traffic.

2. AWS Security Fundamentals

2.1 Defining Cloud Security

Cloud security encompasses a range of practices designed to protect data, applications, and services in the cloud. Key components include:

- **Data Protection:** Ensuring the confidentiality, integrity, and availability of data.
- **Identity and Access Management:** Controlling user access to resources based on roles and permissions.
- **Compliance:** Meeting regulatory requirements and industry standards related to data security.

2.2 The Shared Responsibility Model

AWS operates under a shared responsibility model, which outlines the division of security responsibilities between AWS and the customer. Key aspects include:

- **AWS Responsibilities:** AWS is responsible for the security of the cloud infrastructure, including the physical data centers and network.
- **Customer Responsibilities:** Customers are responsible for securing their applications, data, and configurations within the AWS environment.

3. AWS Networking Services

3.1 Amazon VPC

Amazon VPC is the cornerstone of AWS networking, allowing users to define their virtual network environment. Key features include:

- **VPC Peering:** Allows communication between two VPCs in the same or different AWS accounts.
- **VPC Endpoints:** Enable private connectivity to AWS services without traversing the public internet.

3.1.1 Creating a VPC

- **Step-by-Step Guide:** Instructions for creating a VPC, configuring subnets, route tables, and internet gateways.

3.2 AWS Direct Connect

AWS Direct Connect provides dedicated network connections between on-premises data centers and AWS. Key benefits include:

- **Reduced Latency:** Offers consistent, low-latency network performance.
- **Increased Bandwidth:** Enables higher data transfer rates compared to typical internet connections.

3.2.1 Setting Up AWS Direct Connect

- **Configuration Steps:** Guidance on establishing a Direct Connect connection and configuring virtual interfaces.

3.3 AWS Transit Gateway

AWS Transit Gateway simplifies network management by enabling users to connect multiple VPCs and on-premises networks through a single gateway. Key features include:

- **Centralized Management:** Streamlines the connectivity and routing of multiple VPCs and accounts.
- **Scalable Architecture:** Supports thousands of VPCs and simplifies network design.

3.3.1 Configuring Transit Gateway

- **Implementation Steps:** Instructions for creating and configuring a Transit Gateway and attaching VPCs.

4. Security Measures in AWS

4.1 Identity and Access Management (IAM)

AWS IAM is a critical component for managing user access and permissions. Key features include:

- **User and Group Management:** Create IAM users and groups to manage access to AWS resources.
- **Policies and Roles:** Define fine-grained permissions using policies attached to users, groups, or roles.

4.1.1 Best Practices for IAM

- **Implementing the Principle of Least Privilege:** Grant users only the permissions they need.
- **Regularly Reviewing IAM Policies:** Conduct periodic audits of IAM roles and policies to ensure compliance.

4.2 AWS Key Management Service (KMS)

AWS KMS allows users to create and manage encryption keys for their applications. Key features include:

- **Centralized Key Management:** Provides a centralized interface for managing encryption keys.
- **Integrated Encryption:** Works seamlessly with other AWS services for data encryption.

4.2.1 Implementing KMS for Data Security

- **Creating and Managing Keys:** Step-by-step guidance on creating and managing encryption keys in KMS.

4.3 AWS CloudTrail

AWS CloudTrail is essential for monitoring API activity in AWS accounts. Key benefits include:

- **Event Logging:** Automatically logs API calls made on the AWS account.
- **Audit and Compliance:** Provides visibility into account activity for compliance purposes.

4.3.1 Configuring CloudTrail

- **Setting Up CloudTrail:** Instructions for enabling CloudTrail and configuring log delivery.

5. Securing AWS Networking

5.1 Network Access Control Lists (NACLs)

NACLs provide an additional layer of security at the subnet level. Key features include:

- **Inbound and Outbound Rules:** Control traffic flow to and from subnets using allow/deny rules.
- **Stateless Filtering:** NACLs are stateless, meaning return traffic must be explicitly allowed.

5.1.1 Configuring NACLs

- **Setting Up NACLs:** Step-by-step instructions for creating and configuring NACLs in a VPC.

5.2 Security Groups

Security groups act as virtual firewalls for EC2 instances, controlling inbound and outbound traffic. Key characteristics include:

- **Stateful Filtering:** If an inbound request is allowed, the corresponding outbound response is automatically allowed.
- **Flexible Rules:** Easily add or modify rules to manage traffic.

5.2.1 Best Practices for Security Groups

- **Restricting Access:** Implement security group rules that restrict access based on IP addresses and ports.
- **Monitoring Changes:** Regularly review security group rules to ensure they align with security policies.

6. Advanced Security Practices

6.1 Implementing Multi-Factor Authentication (MFA)

MFA adds an additional layer of security by requiring users to provide two or more verification factors. Key benefits include:

- **Enhanced Security:** Protects accounts from unauthorized access even if credentials are compromised.

- **Flexible Options:** Supports virtual MFA devices, SMS, and hardware tokens.

6.1.1 Setting Up MFA

- **Enabling MFA for IAM Users:** Step-by-step instructions for enabling MFA for AWS IAM users.

6.2 Data Encryption Strategies
Encryption is critical for protecting sensitive data both at rest and in transit. Strategies include:

- **Encrypting Data at Rest:** Use AWS KMS to manage encryption keys for services like S3, EBS, and RDS.
- **Encrypting Data in Transit:** Implement TLS/SSL for data transmitted between applications and AWS services.

6.2.1 Best Practices for Encryption

- **Using Encryption by Default:** Ensure that encryption is enabled for all sensitive data stores.
- **Regularly Rotating Keys:** Implement key rotation policies to enhance security.

7. Monitoring and Auditing Security

7.1 Continuous Monitoring with AWS CloudWatch
CloudWatch provides monitoring and logging capabilities to track security-related metrics. Key features include:

- **Custom Metrics:** Monitor specific metrics related to security, such as unauthorized API calls or changes to IAM policies.
- **Alarms and Notifications:** Set up alarms to trigger notifications for

suspicious activities.

7.1.1 Implementing CloudWatch for Security Monitoring

- **Creating Custom Alarms:** Step-by-step instructions for creating alarms based on security metrics.

7.2 AWS Security Hub

AWS Security Hub provides a comprehensive view of security alerts and compliance status across AWS accounts. Key benefits include:

- **Centralized Security Management:** Aggregate security findings from multiple AWS services.
- **Compliance Checks:** Continuous monitoring for compliance with security best practices.

7.2.1 Configuring Security Hub

- **Setting Up Security Hub:** Instructions for enabling AWS Security Hub and integrating it with other security services.

8. Case Study: Securing an E-commerce Platform on AWS

8.1 Overview of the E-commerce Platform

This case study examines how an e-commerce platform implemented security measures to protect customer data and ensure compliance. Key objectives included:

- **Securing payment information.**
- **Maintaining customer trust and compliance with industry regulations.**

8.2 Architectural Overview and Initial Challenges

Discuss the initial architecture of the e-commerce platform and security challenges faced:

- **Legacy Security Measures:** Initial reliance on outdated security practices that posed risks.
- **Data Compliance Needs:** Need to comply with PCI DSS regulations for handling payment data.

8.3 Security Measures Implemented

Detail the security measures implemented, including:

- **Implementing VPCs and Security Groups:** Configured a VPC with strict security groups to control access to resources.
- **Data Encryption and Key Management:** Used KMS to encrypt sensitive customer data at rest.

8.4 Results and Lessons Learned

Summarize the outcomes of the security implementation, highlighting:

- **Enhanced Security Posture:** Improved security practices led to better protection of customer data.
- **Increased Compliance:** Successfully met regulatory compliance requirements.

Conclusion

In this chapter, we explored the critical aspects of networking and security in AWS. We covered key AWS networking services, security measures, advanced security practices, and real-world case studies that demonstrate effective security implementations. Understanding and applying these concepts are essential for protecting applications and data in the cloud.

In the next chapter, we will focus on **"Automation and Infrastructure as Code,"** discussing strategies for automating infrastructure deployment and management using AWS services like CloudFormation and Terraform.

Chapter 10: Automation and Infrastructure as Code in AWS

Overview

As organizations migrate to the cloud, the need for efficient, repeatable, and reliable deployment processes becomes critical. Automation and Infrastructure as Code (IaC) enable teams to manage their infrastructure using code, significantly reducing the potential for human error while increasing deployment speed and consistency. This chapter explores the principles of automation and IaC, key AWS services, best practices, and real-world applications to achieve operational excellence in the cloud.

1. Understanding Infrastructure as Code (IaC)

1.1 Defining Infrastructure as Code

Infrastructure as Code is the practice of managing and provisioning computing infrastructure through machine-readable definition files, rather than through physical hardware configuration or interactive configuration tools. Key aspects include:

- **Declarative vs. Imperative Approaches:**
- **Declarative:** You specify the desired state of the infrastructure, and the IaC tool manages the process of achieving that state (e.g., AWS CloudFormation).
- **Imperative:** You specify the exact steps required to achieve a desired state (e.g., scripts using AWS CLI).

1.2 Benefits of IaC

Implementing IaC offers several advantages, including:

- **Consistency and Repeatability:** By defining infrastructure in code, deployments become consistent and repeatable, minimizing configuration drift.
- **Version Control:** Infrastructure configurations can be stored in version control systems, enabling tracking of changes and easy rollback.
- **Faster Deployments:** Automating infrastructure provisioning speeds up deployment times, allowing teams to respond quickly to changing business needs.

2. AWS Services for Infrastructure as Code

2.1 AWS CloudFormation

AWS CloudFormation is a core service for implementing IaC on AWS. It allows users to define and provision AWS infrastructure using JSON or YAML templates. Key features include:

- **Template Structure:** CloudFormation templates describe the resources to be provisioned, including their configurations and relationships.
- **Stack Management:** Users can create, update, or delete groups of resources as a single unit known as a stack.

2.1.1 Creating a CloudFormation Template

- **Template Anatomy:** Understand the structure of a CloudFormation template, including parameters, resources, and outputs.
- **Sample Template:** Provide a simple example of a CloudFormation template to create an S3 bucket.

2.2 AWS CDK (Cloud Development Kit)

AWS CDK allows developers to define cloud infrastructure using familiar programming languages, such as JavaScript, Python, or Java. Key benefits include:

- **Programmatic Constructs:** Developers can use programming constructs to define resources, making it easier to integrate with existing codebases.
- **Higher-Level Abstractions:** CDK provides higher-level abstractions for AWS services, simplifying the definition of complex architectures.

2.2.1 Getting Started with AWS CDK

- **Setting Up the CDK Environment:** Step-by-step instructions for setting up a CDK environment and installing required dependencies.
- **Creating a Simple CDK App:** Guide to creating a simple AWS CDK application that provisions an S3 bucket.

2.3 AWS OpsWorks

AWS OpsWorks is a configuration management service that provides managed instances of Chef and Puppet. Key features include:

- **Layered Architecture:** Allows users to define layers of applications and manage the deployment and configuration of those layers.
- **Integration with EC2:** OpsWorks works seamlessly with Amazon EC2 to provision and manage instances.

2.3.1 Using OpsWorks for Configuration Management

- **Creating an OpsWorks Stack:** Instructions for creating and managing an OpsWorks stack and defining application layers.
- **Deploying Applications:** How to deploy applications using OpsWorks and manage configurations.

3. Best Practices for Implementing IaC

3.1 Organizing IaC Code

Organizing infrastructure code is crucial for maintainability and collaboration. Best practices include:

- **Modularization:** Break down infrastructure into reusable modules to promote code reuse and clarity.
- **Naming Conventions:** Use consistent naming conventions for resources and files to enhance readability.

3.2 Version Control for IaC

Using version control systems (VCS) for IaC code provides several benefits:

- **Change Tracking:** Track changes to infrastructure over time, allowing for auditing and rollback if necessary.
- **Collaborative Development:** Enable multiple team members to collaborate on infrastructure code seamlessly.

3.2.1 Integrating IaC with Git

- **Setting Up a Git Repository:** Instructions for creating a Git repository for managing IaC code.
- **Branching Strategies:** Discuss various branching strategies for managing infrastructure code changes.

3.3 Continuous Integration and Continuous Deployment (CI/CD)

Implementing CI/CD pipelines for IaC enables automated testing and deployment of infrastructure changes. Key practices include:

- **Automated Testing:** Use tools like Taskcat or cfn-lint to validate CloudFormation templates before deployment.
- **Pipeline Automation:** Integrate IaC code into CI/CD pipelines using AWS CodePipeline and AWS CodeBuild.

3.3.1 Building a CI/CD Pipeline for IaC

- **Setting Up a CodePipeline:** Step-by-step guide for creating a CI/CD pipeline that automatically deploys infrastructure changes.
- **Integrating CodeBuild:** Instructions for integrating AWS CodeBuild to validate and test IaC templates.

4. Advanced Automation Techniques

4.1 Using AWS Lambda for Automation

AWS Lambda can be leveraged to automate various tasks related to IaC and infrastructure management. Key use cases include:

- **Event-Driven Automation:** Trigger Lambda functions based on events, such as changes in S3 or CloudTrail logs.
- **Resource Cleanup:** Use Lambda functions to automate resource cleanup tasks, such as deleting unused resources.

4.1.1 Creating a Lambda Function for Automation

- **Step-by-Step Instructions:** Guide on creating a simple Lambda function that automates an AWS task.

4.2 Implementing Monitoring and Logging for IaC

Monitoring and logging infrastructure changes is essential for identifying issues and maintaining compliance. Best practices include:

- **CloudTrail Integration:** Ensure that all changes made through IaC tools are logged by enabling AWS CloudTrail.
- **Config Rules:** Use AWS Config rules to monitor compliance with defined best practices.

4.2.1 Setting Up CloudTrail for Monitoring

- **Enabling CloudTrail:** Instructions for setting up AWS CloudTrail to monitor changes in infrastructure.

5. Security Considerations in IaC

5.1 Securing IaC Code

Securing infrastructure code is critical for preventing unauthorized access and vulnerabilities. Key practices include:

- **Access Control:** Implement IAM policies to control who can modify infrastructure code.
- **Secrets Management:** Use AWS Secrets Manager or Parameter Store to manage sensitive information in IaC code.

5.1.1 Best Practices for Managing Secrets

- **Integrating Secrets Manager:** Step-by-step instructions for using Secrets Manager with CloudFormation templates.

5.2 Auditing and Compliance for IaC

Organizations must ensure that their infrastructure code complies with security policies and regulations. Key strategies include:

- **Static Code Analysis:** Use tools like Checkov or tfsec to analyze IaC code for security vulnerabilities before deployment.
- **Compliance Checks:** Implement compliance checks in CI/CD pipelines

to ensure adherence to policies.

6. Real-World Case Study: Automating Infrastructure Deployment for a SaaS Application

6.1 Overview of the SaaS Application

This case study examines how a Software as a Service (SaaS) company automated its infrastructure deployment using IaC in AWS. Key objectives included:

- **Streamlining deployment processes.**
- **Improving team collaboration and efficiency.**

6.2 Architectural Overview and Initial Challenges

Discuss the initial architecture of the SaaS application and challenges faced:

- **Manual Provisioning:** Initial reliance on manual provisioning processes led to inconsistencies and errors.
- **Difficulty in Scaling:** Scaling the infrastructure became cumbersome and time-consuming.

6.3 Implementing Automation with IaC

Detail the automation strategies employed, including:

- **Adopting CloudFormation:** Transitioning to AWS CloudFormation for defining infrastructure.
- **Integrating CI/CD Pipelines:** Establishing CI/CD pipelines using CodePipeline and CodeBuild for automated deployments.

6.4 Results and Lessons Learned

Summarize the outcomes of the automation implementation, highlighting:

- **Faster Deployment Times:** Achieved significant reductions in deployment times and increased reliability.

- **Enhanced Collaboration:** Improved collaboration among development and operations teams through version-controlled infrastructure code.

Conclusion

In this chapter, we explored the critical aspects of automation and Infrastructure as Code (IaC) in AWS. We covered key AWS services for IaC, best practices for implementing automation, advanced techniques for enhancing IaC, and real-world case studies that illustrate effective automation strategies. Understanding and applying these concepts is essential for organizations to achieve operational excellence and agility in the cloud.

In the next chapter, we will focus on **"Cost Management and Optimization in AWS,"** discussing strategies and tools to monitor and optimize AWS costs while maintaining performance and scalability.

Chapter 11: Cloud Migration Strategies and Best Practices

Overview

As organizations increasingly adopt cloud technologies, migrating applications and workloads to the cloud has become a crucial step in their digital transformation journey. Effective migration strategies ensure that businesses can leverage the benefits of the cloud—such as scalability, cost efficiency, and enhanced performance—while minimizing risks and disruptions. This chapter explores the different migration strategies, AWS services that facilitate migration, best practices, and real-world case studies to provide a comprehensive understanding of cloud migration.

1. Understanding Cloud Migration

1.1 Defining Cloud Migration

Cloud migration refers to the process of moving applications, data, and workloads from on-premises infrastructure or other cloud environments to the cloud. It involves various activities, including:

- **Assessment of Existing Infrastructure:** Evaluating the current envi-

ronment to determine what needs to be migrated and how.
- **Planning and Strategy Development:** Creating a roadmap for migration, including timelines, resources, and responsibilities.
- **Execution of Migration Activities:** Implementing the migration plan through the actual transfer of applications and data.

1.2 Benefits of Cloud Migration

Migrating to the cloud offers numerous advantages, including:

- **Cost Savings:** Reducing capital expenditures by eliminating the need for physical hardware and maintenance.
- **Scalability:** Quickly adjusting resources to meet changing demands without significant lead time.
- **Enhanced Performance:** Leveraging the latest cloud technologies and services to improve application performance and reliability.
- **Increased Agility:** Rapidly deploying new applications and services to respond to business needs.

2. Cloud Migration Strategies

2.1 The 6 R's of Cloud Migration

Organizations can choose from various migration strategies, often referred to as the "6 R's": Rehost, Replatform, Refactor, Repurchase, Retire, and Retain.

- **Rehost (Lift and Shift):** Moving applications to the cloud without significant modifications. This is often the quickest method for migration.
- **Example:** Migrating a virtual machine (VM) running on-premises to an EC2 instance in AWS.
- **Replatform (Lift, Tinker, and Shift):** Making minor optimizations to the application during migration. This could involve changing the underlying database or using managed services.
- **Example:** Migrating a web application from a VM to an AWS Elastic Beanstalk environment.

- **Refactor (Re-architect):** Redesigning the application to take advantage of cloud-native features. This often requires more development effort but can lead to significant performance and cost benefits.
- **Example:** Rewriting a monolithic application into microservices hosted on AWS Fargate.
- **Repurchase:** Replacing an existing application with a SaaS solution. This strategy often reduces maintenance costs and provides modern features.
- **Example:** Migrating from a traditional CRM system to Salesforce.
- **Retire:** Identifying and eliminating applications that are no longer useful. This helps streamline the application portfolio.
- **Example:** Decommissioning legacy applications that have been replaced by more efficient solutions.
- **Retain:** Keeping certain applications on-premises due to specific requirements such as compliance or performance needs.
- **Example:** Retaining an on-premises database that cannot be migrated due to regulatory restrictions.

2.2 Choosing the Right Migration Strategy

Choosing the appropriate migration strategy depends on several factors:

- **Business Objectives:** Align migration goals with overall business strategies and priorities.
- **Application Dependencies:** Assess how applications interact with each other and their dependencies on other systems.
- **Cost Considerations:** Evaluate the costs associated with each migration approach, including potential savings and ROI.

3. AWS Migration Services

3.1 AWS Migration Hub

AWS Migration Hub provides a central location to track the progress of application migrations across multiple AWS and partner solutions. Key features include:

- **Migration Tracking:** Visualize migration progress and gather insights on different migration projects.
- **Integration with AWS Services:** Works seamlessly with services like AWS Application Discovery Service and AWS Server Migration Service.

3.2 AWS Application Discovery Service

AWS Application Discovery Service helps organizations plan their migration by collecting usage and configuration data from on-premises servers. Key benefits include:

- **Automated Discovery:** Automatically gathers information about existing applications and their dependencies.
- **Dependency Mapping:** Visualizes application dependencies to facilitate migration planning.

3.2.1 Setting Up Application Discovery Service

- **Configuring the Agent:** Step-by-step instructions on installing and configuring the AWS Application Discovery Service agent on on-premises servers.

3.3 AWS Server Migration Service (SMS)

AWS SMS is a service that automates the migration of on-premises workloads to AWS. Key features include:

- **Incremental Replication:** Allows for incremental updates to minimize downtime during migration.
- **Scheduling Migrations:** Users can schedule and automate migration tasks for better planning.

3.3.1 Using Server Migration Service

- **Creating a Migration Job:** Instructions for setting up and executing a migration job using AWS SMS.

3.4 AWS Database Migration Service (DMS)

AWS DMS helps migrate databases to AWS quickly and securely. Key features include:

- **Heterogeneous Migration:** Supports migrations between different database platforms, such as Oracle to Aurora.
- **Continuous Data Replication:** Enables ongoing replication during migration to minimize downtime.

3.4.1 Migrating Databases with DMS

- **Setting Up a DMS Task:** Step-by-step guidance for creating a database migration task using AWS DMS.

4. Best Practices for Cloud Migration

4.1 Planning and Assessment

A thorough assessment and planning phase is crucial for a successful migration. Key practices include:

- **Conducting a Cloud Readiness Assessment:** Evaluate existing infrastructure, applications, and workflows to determine suitability for the cloud.
- **Developing a Detailed Migration Plan:** Create a roadmap outlining each phase of the migration, timelines, and resource allocation.

4.2 Executing the Migration

Executing the migration effectively requires careful coordination. Best practices include:

- **Pilot Migrations:** Start with a pilot migration of non-critical applications to test the process and gain insights.
- **Monitoring Performance:** Continuously monitor performance during migration to identify and address any issues that arise.

4.3 Post-Migration Optimization

After migration, organizations should focus on optimizing their cloud environment. Key practices include:

- **Cost Optimization:** Review resource utilization and implement cost-saving measures such as auto-scaling and rightsizing.
- **Security Review:** Conduct a security assessment to ensure that applications and data are protected in the cloud.

5. Advanced Migration Techniques

5.1 Automated Migration Tools

Utilizing automated migration tools can streamline the migration process. Key tools include:

- **AWS CloudEndure Migration:** A disaster recovery tool that facilitates continuous replication of applications and data to AWS.
- **Third-Party Migration Solutions:** Various partners provide specialized migration tools that may enhance specific migration scenarios.

5.1.1 Using CloudEndure for Migration

- **Setting Up CloudEndure:** Instructions for configuring and using CloudEndure for automated application migration.

5.2 Hybrid Migration Strategies

For organizations transitioning to the cloud, hybrid migration strategies can ease the process. Key considerations include:

- **Phased Migration:** Gradually migrating applications while maintaining some workloads on-premises until fully transitioned.
- **Multi-Cloud Strategies:** Leveraging multiple cloud providers for redundancy and flexibility.

6. Real-World Case Study: Migrating a Legacy Application to AWS

6.1 Overview of the Legacy Application

This case study examines the migration of a legacy application to AWS. Key objectives included:

- **Modernizing the application architecture.**
- **Improving scalability and reliability.**

6.2 Architectural Overview and Initial Challenges

Discuss the initial architecture of the legacy application and challenges faced:

- **Tightly Coupled Architecture:** Initial design made it difficult to scale and integrate with modern systems.
- **High Maintenance Costs:** Maintaining legacy infrastructure was costly and resource-intensive.

6.3 Migration Strategy Implemented

Detail the migration strategy employed, including:

- **Choosing the Replatform Strategy:** Migrating the application to AWS Elastic Beanstalk to take advantage of managed services.
- **Utilizing DMS for Database Migration:** Leveraging AWS DMS to migrate the backend database to Amazon RDS.

6.4 Results and Lessons Learned

Summarize the outcomes of the migration, highlighting:

- **Improved Performance:** Achieved significant performance improvements post-migration.
- **Enhanced Scalability:** The application could now scale automatically based on demand.

7. Tools and Resources for Migration

7.1 AWS Migration Hub

AWS Migration Hub provides a single location for tracking the progress of application migrations. Key features include:

- **Centralized View:** Monitor migration progress across various AWS services and third-party tools.
- **Integration with Other Tools:** Works with other AWS migration services to provide a holistic view of the migration process.

7.2 AWS Documentation and Training

AWS offers a wealth of documentation, training resources, and best practices for migration. Key resources include:

- **AWS Whitepapers:** In-depth technical documentation covering various aspects of cloud migration.
- **AWS Training and Certification:** Courses designed to provide hands-on experience with AWS migration tools and services.

8. Conclusion

In this chapter, we explored the critical aspects of cloud migration strategies and best practices. We covered the various migration strategies, AWS services that facilitate migration, best practices for planning and executing migrations, and real-world case studies that demonstrate effective migration implementations. Understanding and applying these concepts are essential for organizations looking to successfully migrate to the AWS cloud and fully leverage its benefits.

In the next chapter, we will focus on **"Data Management and Analytics in AWS,"** discussing strategies and services for efficiently managing and analyzing data in the cloud.

Chapter 12: Networking and Security Best Practices in AWS

Overview

As organizations increasingly adopt cloud technologies, networking and security have become paramount to successful cloud architecture. AWS provides a robust suite of networking services that enable organizations to connect their resources securely and efficiently. This chapter explores the principles of networking in AWS, key security measures, best practices for securing cloud networks, and strategies to ensure data protection.

1. Understanding AWS Networking Concepts

1.1 Overview of Networking in AWS

AWS networking services allow organizations to build and manage secure, scalable, and highly available network architectures. Key components include:

- **Virtual Private Cloud (VPC):** A logically isolated section of the AWS cloud where users can define their network environment.

- **Subnets:** Segments of a VPC that allow for organization and security of resources.
- **Internet Gateways and NAT Gateways:** Enable communication between instances in a VPC and the internet.

1.2 Key Components of AWS Networking

Understanding the core components of AWS networking is essential for building secure architectures:

- **VPC Peering:** Allows two VPCs to communicate with each other as if they are on the same network.
- **Route Tables:** Determine how traffic is directed within a VPC and between subnets.
- **Network ACLs:** Control inbound and outbound traffic at the subnet level, providing an additional layer of security.

2. Designing Secure VPCs

2.1 Creating a Secure VPC Architecture

When designing a secure VPC architecture, consider the following best practices:

- **Isolation of Resources:** Use separate VPCs for different environments (e.g., development, testing, production) to minimize risk.
- **Public and Private Subnets:** Implement public subnets for resources that require internet access (e.g., web servers) and private subnets for databases and application servers.

2.1.1 Setting Up a VPC

- **Step-by-Step Guide:** Instructions for creating a VPC with public and private subnets, including configuring route tables and security groups.

2.2 Implementing Security Groups

Security groups act as virtual firewalls for EC2 instances, controlling inbound and outbound traffic. Key features include:

- **Stateful Filtering:** If an inbound request is allowed, the corresponding outbound response is automatically allowed.
- **Flexible Rules:** Easily add or modify rules to manage traffic.

2.2.1 Best Practices for Security Groups

- **Restricting Access:** Implement security group rules that restrict access based on IP addresses and ports.
- **Monitoring Changes:** Regularly review security group rules to ensure they align with security policies.

3. Data Protection in AWS

3.1 Data Encryption Strategies

Data encryption is critical for protecting sensitive information both at rest and in transit. Strategies include:

- **Encrypting Data at Rest:** Use AWS KMS to manage encryption keys for services like S3, EBS, and RDS.
- **Encrypting Data in Transit:** Implement TLS/SSL for data transmitted between applications and AWS services.

3.1.1 Best Practices for Encryption

- **Using Encryption by Default:** Ensure that encryption is enabled for all sensitive data stores.
- **Regularly Rotating Keys:** Implement key rotation policies to enhance security.

3.2 AWS Key Management Service (KMS)

AWS KMS is a fully managed service that simplifies the process of creating and controlling the encryption keys used to encrypt data. Key features include:

- **Centralized Key Management:** Provides a centralized interface for managing encryption keys.
- **Integrated Encryption:** Works seamlessly with other AWS services for data encryption.

3.2.1 Configuring KMS for Data Security

- **Creating and Managing Keys:** Instructions for creating and managing encryption keys in KMS.

4. Identity and Access Management (IAM)

4.1 Overview of AWS IAM

AWS Identity and Access Management (IAM) enables you to manage access to AWS services and resources securely. Key features include:

- **User and Group Management:** Create IAM users and groups to manage access to AWS resources.
- **Policies and Roles:** Define fine-grained permissions using policies attached to users, groups, or roles.

4.2 Best Practices for IAM

To enhance security in AWS, implement the following IAM best practices:

- **Implementing the Principle of Least Privilege:** Grant users only the permissions they need to perform their job functions.
- **Regularly Reviewing IAM Policies:** Conduct periodic audits of IAM roles and policies to ensure compliance.

4.2.1 Multi-Factor Authentication (MFA)

Enabling MFA adds an extra layer of security by requiring users to provide two or more verification factors. Key benefits include:

- **Enhanced Security:** Protects accounts from unauthorized access even if credentials are compromised.
- **Flexible Options:** Supports virtual MFA devices, SMS, and hardware tokens.

5. Monitoring and Logging for Security

5.1 Continuous Monitoring with AWS CloudWatch

AWS CloudWatch provides monitoring capabilities to track security-related metrics. Key features include:

- **Custom Metrics:** Monitor specific metrics related to security, such as unauthorized API calls or changes to IAM policies.
- **Alarms and Notifications:** Set up alarms to trigger notifications for suspicious activities.

5.1.1 Implementing CloudWatch for Security Monitoring

- **Creating Custom Alarms:** Step-by-step instructions for creating alarms based on security metrics.

5.2 AWS CloudTrail

AWS CloudTrail is essential for monitoring API activity in AWS accounts. Key benefits include:

- **Event Logging:** Automatically logs API calls made on the AWS account.
- **Audit and Compliance:** Provides visibility into account activity for compliance purposes.

5.2.1 Configuring CloudTrail

- **Setting Up CloudTrail:** Instructions for enabling CloudTrail and configuring log delivery.

6. Network Security Best Practices

6.1 Implementing Network Access Control Lists (NACLs)

NACLs provide an additional layer of security at the subnet level. Key features include:

- **Inbound and Outbound Rules:** Control traffic flow to and from subnets using allow/deny rules.
- **Stateless Filtering:** NACLs are stateless, meaning return traffic must be explicitly allowed.

6.1.1 Configuring NACLs

- **Setting Up NACLs:** Step-by-step instructions for creating and configuring NACLs in a VPC.

6.2 Using AWS Web Application Firewall (WAF)

AWS WAF helps protect applications from web exploits and attacks. Key features include:

- **Custom Rules:** Create rules to filter out malicious traffic based on patterns, IP addresses, and request attributes.
- **Integration with CloudFront:** WAF can be integrated with Amazon CloudFront for enhanced protection.

6.2.1 Configuring AWS WAF

- **Setting Up WAF Rules:** Instructions for configuring WAF rules to protect web applications.

7. Advanced Security Measures

7.1 Implementing AWS Security Hub

AWS Security Hub provides a comprehensive view of security alerts and compliance status across AWS accounts. Key benefits include:

- **Centralized Security Management:** Aggregate security findings from multiple AWS services.
- **Compliance Checks:** Continuous monitoring for compliance with security best practices.

7.1.1 Configuring Security Hub

- **Setting Up Security Hub:** Instructions for enabling AWS Security Hub and integrating it with other security services.

7.2 Using Amazon GuardDuty

Amazon GuardDuty is a threat detection service that continuously monitors for malicious activity and unauthorized behavior. Key features include:

- **Intelligent Threat Detection:** Uses machine learning and threat intelligence to identify potential security threats.
- **Automated Alerts:** Sends alerts when potential security issues are detected.

7.2.1 Implementing GuardDuty

- **Setting Up GuardDuty:** Step-by-step instructions for enabling and configuring Amazon GuardDuty.

8. Compliance and Governance in AWS

8.1 Understanding Compliance Requirements

Compliance in the cloud involves adhering to legal, regulatory, and industry standards regarding data protection and security. Organizations must ensure that their cloud practices align with applicable regulations, such as:

- **General Data Protection Regulation (GDPR)**
- **Health Insurance Portability and Accountability Act (HIPAA)**
- **Payment Card Industry Data Security Standard (PCI DSS)**

8.2 AWS Compliance Programs

AWS provides a wide range of compliance certifications and attestations to help customers meet regulatory requirements. Key compliance programs include:

- **ISO Certifications:** AWS is ISO 27001 certified, demonstrating its commitment to information security management.
- **SOC Reports:** AWS regularly undergoes independent audits to assess controls and processes against SOC 1, SOC 2, and SOC 3 standards.
- **HIPAA Compliance:** AWS offers services compliant with HIPAA, enabling healthcare organizations to store and process sensitive medical data securely.

8.2.1 Implementing Compliance Controls in AWS

To implement compliance controls in AWS, organizations should:

- **Use AWS Artifact:** A self-service portal that provides on-demand access to AWS compliance documentation and reports.
- **Enable CloudTrail for Audit Trails:** Use AWS CloudTrail to maintain audit logs of all API calls and activities in the AWS account.

9. Case Study: Securing an E-commerce Platform on AWS

9.1 Overview of the E-commerce Platform

This case study examines how an e-commerce platform implemented security measures to protect customer data and ensure compliance. Key objectives included:

- **Securing payment information.**
- **Maintaining customer trust and compliance with industry regulations.**

9.2 Architectural Overview and Initial Challenges

Discuss the initial architecture of the e-commerce platform and security challenges faced:

- **Legacy Security Measures:** Initial reliance on outdated security practices that posed risks.
- **Data Compliance Needs:** Need to comply with PCI DSS regulations for handling payment data.

9.3 Security Measures Implemented

Detail the security measures implemented, including:

- **Implementing VPCs and Security Groups:** Configured a VPC with strict security groups to control access to resources.
- **Data Encryption and Key Management:** Used KMS to encrypt sensitive customer data at rest.

9.4 Results and Lessons Learned

Summarize the outcomes of the security implementation, highlighting:

- **Enhanced Security Posture:** Improved security practices led to better protection of customer data.

- **Increased Compliance:** Successfully met regulatory compliance requirements.

10. Conclusion

In this chapter, we explored the critical aspects of networking and security best practices in AWS. We covered key AWS networking services, security measures, advanced security practices, and real-world case studies that demonstrate effective security implementations. Understanding and applying these concepts are essential for protecting applications and data in the cloud.

In the next chapter, we will focus on **"Data Management and Analytics in AWS,"** discussing strategies and services for efficiently managing and analyzing data in the cloud.

Chapter 13: Data Management and Analytics in AWS

Overview

Data has become a pivotal asset for organizations, driving insights, decision-making, and innovation. With the exponential growth of data generated every day, businesses need robust data management and analytics strategies to harness the full potential of their information. AWS provides a comprehensive suite of services designed for effective data management, storage, and analysis. This chapter explores best practices for managing data in AWS, the various services available for data analytics, and strategies for building a data-driven culture.

1. Understanding Data Management

1.1 What is Data Management?

Data management encompasses a set of practices, policies, and procedures that govern the acquisition, storage, organization, and utilization of data. Key components include:

- **Data Governance:** Ensuring data quality, privacy, and compliance with regulations.

- **Data Integration:** Combining data from various sources for a unified view.
- **Data Security:** Protecting data from unauthorized access and breaches.
- **Data Lifecycle Management:** Managing data from creation to deletion, ensuring relevance and compliance.

1.2 The Importance of Data Management

Effective data management is crucial for several reasons:

- **Informed Decision-Making:** High-quality data enables better analysis and more informed business decisions.
- **Operational Efficiency:** Streamlined data processes reduce redundancy and improve workflow.
- **Regulatory Compliance:** Proper management ensures compliance with data-related regulations such as GDPR, HIPAA, and others.
- **Enhanced Data Security:** Implementing robust data management practices enhances data protection and minimizes risks.

2. Data Storage Solutions in AWS

2.1 Amazon S3 (Simple Storage Service)

Amazon S3 is an object storage service that offers industry-leading scalability, data availability, and security. Key features include:

- **Durability:** S3 is designed for 99.999999999% durability, ensuring data integrity.
- **Scalability:** Automatically scales to accommodate growing data needs without pre-provisioning.
- **Cost Management:** Offers various storage classes, such as S3 Standard, S3 Intelligent-Tiering, and S3 Glacier, to optimize costs based on access patterns.

2.1.1 Best Practices for Using Amazon S3

- **Implement Versioning:** Enable versioning to maintain historical versions of objects, protecting against accidental deletions.
- **Utilize Lifecycle Policies:** Set up lifecycle rules to transition objects to lower-cost storage classes as they age.
- **Data Encryption:** Use server-side encryption (SSE) to encrypt data at rest, and utilize SSL/TLS for data in transit.

2.2 Amazon RDS (Relational Database Service)

Amazon RDS simplifies the setup, operation, and scaling of relational databases in the cloud. Key features include:

- **Multi-AZ Deployments:** Provides high availability and automatic failover to a standby instance in another Availability Zone.
- **Automated Backups:** Automatically backs up databases, allowing for point-in-time recovery.

2.2.1 Choosing the Right Database Engine

Amazon RDS supports various database engines, including MySQL, PostgreSQL, Oracle, and SQL Server. Selecting the right engine depends on:

- **Use Case Requirements:** Consider the application's specific needs, such as transaction processing or analytics.
- **Familiarity and Expertise:** Leverage existing knowledge and expertise within the organization.

2.3 Amazon DynamoDB

Amazon DynamoDB is a fully managed NoSQL database service designed for high-performance applications. Key features include:

- **Automatic Scaling:** Dynamically adjusts throughput capacity based on traffic demands.

- **Global Tables:** Enable multi-region, fully replicated tables for low-latency access.

2.3.1 Best Practices for Using DynamoDB

- **Use Partition Keys:** Design tables with effective partition keys to distribute workloads evenly.
- **Implement Global Secondary Indexes:** Utilize indexes to support diverse query patterns without duplicating data.
- **Monitor and Optimize Performance:** Use Amazon CloudWatch to monitor performance metrics and adjust capacity as needed.

3. Data Analytics Services in AWS

3.1 Amazon Athena

Amazon Athena is an interactive query service that allows users to analyze data directly in Amazon S3 using standard SQL. Key benefits include:

- **Serverless Architecture:** No infrastructure management required; pay only for the queries you run.
- **Quick Insights:** Provides rapid query responses, enabling data exploration without extensive setup.

3.1.1 Using Athena for Data Analysis

- **Setting Up Athena:** Instructions for creating an Athena database and running SQL queries against data stored in S3.
- **Integrating with AWS Glue:** Utilize AWS Glue to catalog data in S3 and make it discoverable for querying in Athena.

3.2 Amazon Redshift

Amazon Redshift is a fully managed, petabyte-scale data warehouse service. Key features include:

- **High Performance:** Uses columnar storage and parallel processing to deliver fast query performance.
- **Scalability:** Easily scale the data warehouse up or down based on workload demands.

3.2.1 Best Practices for Using Redshift

- **Data Distribution Styles:** Choose the right data distribution style (KEY, ALL, EVEN) to optimize performance.
- **Cluster Maintenance:** Regularly monitor and maintain the cluster for optimal performance, including vacuuming and analyzing tables.
- **Integration with BI Tools:** Connect Redshift to business intelligence tools for data visualization and reporting.

3.3 Amazon QuickSight

Amazon QuickSight is a cloud-powered business intelligence service that makes it easy to create and publish interactive dashboards. Key benefits include:

- **Easy Data Visualization:** Allows users to visualize data through various chart types and dashboards.
- **Embedded Analytics:** Integrate analytics directly into applications for a seamless user experience.

3.3.1 Creating Dashboards in QuickSight

- **Connecting to Data Sources:** Instructions for connecting QuickSight to various data sources, including S3, Redshift, and RDS.
- **Building Interactive Dashboards:** Step-by-step guidance for creating and customizing dashboards in QuickSight.

4. Data Lifecycle Management

4.1 Understanding Data Lifecycle Management

Data lifecycle management (DLM) refers to the policies and processes for managing data throughout its lifecycle—from creation and storage to archiving and deletion. Key practices include:

- **Data Classification:** Categorize data based on its sensitivity and compliance requirements.
- **Retention Policies:** Define retention policies for data based on regulatory requirements and business needs.

4.2 Implementing Data Lifecycle Policies in AWS

AWS offers various services and features to automate data lifecycle management, including:

- **Amazon S3 Lifecycle Policies:** Automate the transition of objects between storage classes or deletion based on defined rules.
- **AWS Backup:** Centralize backup management across AWS services, allowing for automated backup schedules and retention policies.

4.2.1 Setting Up Lifecycle Policies

- **Creating S3 Lifecycle Rules:** Step-by-step instructions for creating lifecycle rules in Amazon S3 to manage data effectively.

5. Data Governance and Security

5.1 Importance of Data Governance

Data governance involves the management of data availability, usability, integrity, and security. It ensures that data is accurate, consistent, and used responsibly. Key components include:

- **Data Stewardship:** Assigning responsibilities for data management and quality.
- **Compliance Monitoring:** Ensuring adherence to data-related regulations and policies.

5.2 Implementing Data Governance in AWS
To implement effective data governance in AWS, organizations should:

- **Establish a Data Governance Framework:** Define roles, responsibilities, and policies for data management.
- **Utilize AWS Lake Formation:** Simplify the process of building and securing data lakes while ensuring data governance.

5.2.1 Setting Up AWS Lake Formation

- **Creating a Data Lake:** Instructions for setting up a data lake using AWS Lake Formation, including data ingestion and access control.

6. Data Analytics Best Practices

6.1 Choosing the Right Analytics Tools
Selecting the appropriate tools for data analytics is crucial for achieving insights. Considerations include:

- **Business Requirements:** Align analytics tools with business goals and user needs.
- **Data Volume and Variety:** Choose tools capable of handling the specific data types and volumes your organization generates.

6.2 Building a Data-Driven Culture
To foster a data-driven culture within an organization, consider the following practices:

- **Encouraging Data Literacy:** Provide training and resources to help employees understand and utilize data effectively.
- **Promoting Collaboration:** Facilitate collaboration between data scientists, analysts, and business stakeholders to drive insights.

6.2.1 Implementing Data Literacy Programs

- **Creating Training Resources:** Develop training materials and workshops to enhance data literacy across the organization.

7. Real-World Case Study: Leveraging Data Analytics for Business Insights

7.1 Overview of the Company
This case study examines how a retail company leveraged AWS data management and analytics services to gain insights and improve decision-making. Key objectives included:

- **Understanding customer behavior.**
- **Optimizing inventory management.**

7.2 Data Architecture and Initial Challenges
Discuss the initial data architecture and challenges faced:

- **Fragmented Data Sources:** Data was scattered across multiple systems, making it difficult to gain insights.
- **Manual Reporting Processes:** Reporting was time-consuming and prone to errors.

7.3 Implementing Data Management and Analytics Solutions
Detail the data management and analytics solutions implemented:

- **Centralizing Data in S3:** Migrated data to Amazon S3 for centralized storage and easy access.

- **Using Redshift for Analytics:** Leveraged Amazon Redshift for data warehousing and analytics.

7.4 Results and Lessons Learned

Summarize the outcomes of the analytics implementation:

- **Improved Decision-Making:** Gained valuable insights into customer behavior, leading to more informed marketing strategies.
- **Increased Operational Efficiency:** Optimized inventory management, resulting in reduced costs and improved customer satisfaction.

8. Conclusion

In this chapter, we explored the critical aspects of data management and analytics in AWS. We covered data storage solutions, AWS services for analytics, best practices for managing data, and real-world case studies that demonstrate effective data management implementations. Understanding and applying these concepts are essential for organizations looking to harness the power of data in the cloud.

In the next chapter, we will focus on **"Machine Learning and AI in AWS,"** discussing how organizations can leverage AWS services to build intelligent applications and drive innovation.

Chapter 14: Machine Learning and AI in AWS

Overview

The advent of machine learning (ML) and artificial intelligence (AI) has revolutionized how organizations operate, enabling them to leverage data for predictive analytics, automation, and enhanced decision-making. AWS offers a comprehensive suite of services and tools designed to simplify the implementation of machine learning and AI solutions. This chapter explores the key concepts of machine learning, the various AWS services available for ML and AI, best practices for implementation, and real-world applications that showcase the transformative potential of these technologies.

1. Understanding Machine Learning and AI

1.1 Defining Machine Learning

Machine Learning is a subset of artificial intelligence that focuses on building systems that can learn from and make decisions based on data. Key aspects include:

- **Supervised Learning:** Involves training models on labeled datasets, allowing them to predict outcomes based on input features (e.g., classification and regression tasks).
- **Unsupervised Learning:** Involves training models on unlabeled data to find patterns and relationships within the data (e.g., clustering).
- **Reinforcement Learning:** Involves training models to make a sequence of decisions by rewarding desired actions and penalizing undesired ones.

1.2 Defining Artificial Intelligence

Artificial Intelligence encompasses a broader range of technologies that simulate human intelligence, including reasoning, learning, problem-solving, perception, and language understanding. Key components include:

- **Natural Language Processing (NLP):** Enables machines to understand and interpret human language.
- **Computer Vision:** Allows machines to interpret and process visual information from the world.

1.3 Importance of Machine Learning and AI

Machine learning and AI provide significant benefits to organizations, including:

- **Data-Driven Insights:** Extract valuable insights from large datasets, driving informed decision-making.
- **Automation:** Streamline operations by automating repetitive tasks, enhancing efficiency.
- **Personalization:** Tailor products and services to individual customer preferences, improving user experiences.

2. Machine Learning Lifecycle

2.1 Understanding the ML Lifecycle

The machine learning lifecycle consists of several stages that guide the development and deployment of ML models. These stages include:

- **Problem Definition:** Clearly define the problem to be solved and the objectives of the ML model.
- **Data Collection:** Gather relevant data from various sources for training and evaluation.
- **Data Preparation:** Clean, preprocess, and transform data to make it suitable for modeling.
- **Model Training:** Train machine learning models using appropriate algorithms and techniques.
- **Model Evaluation:** Assess the performance of the model using evaluation metrics and validation techniques.
- **Model Deployment:** Deploy the model into production, making it available for inference.
- **Monitoring and Maintenance:** Continuously monitor the model's performance and update it as necessary.

3. AWS Services for Machine Learning

3.1 Amazon SageMaker

Amazon SageMaker is a fully managed service that provides tools and capabilities for building, training, and deploying machine learning models. Key features include:

- **Integrated Development Environment (IDE):** Jupyter notebooks for data exploration and model development.
- **Built-in Algorithms:** Pre-built machine learning algorithms that can be easily applied to datasets.
- **Model Training and Tuning:** Automated model training and hyperpa-

rameter tuning to optimize performance.

3.1.1 Getting Started with SageMaker

- **Creating a SageMaker Notebook Instance:** Step-by-step instructions for setting up a notebook instance in Amazon SageMaker.
- **Training a Simple Model:** Guidance on training a basic machine learning model using SageMaker built-in algorithms.

3.2 AWS Deep Learning AMIs

AWS Deep Learning AMIs provide pre-built environments for deep learning applications. Key features include:

- **Pre-installed Frameworks:** Includes popular deep learning frameworks like TensorFlow, PyTorch, and Apache MXNet.
- **Optimized for Performance:** AMIs are optimized for performance on GPU instances.

3.2.1 Using Deep Learning AMIs

- **Launching a Deep Learning Instance:** Instructions for launching an EC2 instance with a deep learning AMI and configuring it for model training.

3.3 Amazon Rekognition

Amazon Rekognition is a service that enables developers to add image and video analysis capabilities to applications. Key features include:

- **Object and Scene Detection:** Identifies objects, scenes, and activities in images and videos.
- **Facial Analysis:** Detects and analyzes faces in images for identification or emotion analysis.

3.3.1 Implementing Rekognition

- **Analyzing Images with Rekognition:** Step-by-step guide on using Amazon Rekognition to analyze images for object detection.

4. Best Practices for Machine Learning on AWS

4.1 Data Preparation and Management
Effective data management is crucial for successful machine learning outcomes. Key practices include:

- **Data Quality:** Ensure that data is accurate, complete, and relevant for the intended analysis.
- **Data Versioning:** Use tools like DVC or Git LFS to track changes in datasets and models over time.

4.2 Model Training and Evaluation
Implementing best practices for model training and evaluation helps improve performance and reliability. Key strategies include:

- **Cross-Validation:** Use techniques like k-fold cross-validation to assess model performance and prevent overfitting.
- **Hyperparameter Tuning:** Utilize automated tools like SageMaker Automatic Model Tuning to optimize hyperparameters effectively.

4.3 Model Deployment and Monitoring
Once a model is trained, deploying it effectively is essential for achieving real-world impact. Best practices include:

- **Version Control for Models:** Maintain version control for models to track changes and facilitate rollbacks if necessary.
- **Monitoring Model Performance:** Use tools like Amazon CloudWatch to monitor model performance and detect anomalies over time.

5. Real-World Use Cases of Machine Learning in AWS

5.1 Retail: Personalized Recommendations
Many retail organizations leverage machine learning to provide personalized product recommendations to customers. Key features include:

- **Collaborative Filtering:** Using customer behavior data to recommend products based on similar users' preferences.
- **Real-Time Analytics:** Analyzing user interactions in real time to adjust recommendations dynamically.

5.1.1 Implementing a Recommendation System

- **Using Amazon Personalize:** Instructions for setting up Amazon Personalize to build and deploy a recommendation system.

5.2 Healthcare: Predictive Analytics
In the healthcare sector, machine learning is used for predictive analytics to improve patient outcomes. Key applications include:

- **Disease Prediction:** Analyzing patient data to predict the likelihood of diseases and complications.
- **Treatment Recommendations:** Providing tailored treatment options based on historical patient outcomes.

5.2.1 Implementing Predictive Analytics

- **Using SageMaker for Predictive Models:** Guidance on using Amazon SageMaker to build and deploy predictive models for healthcare applications.

5.3 Finance: Fraud Detection
Financial institutions utilize machine learning for real-time fraud detection

and risk assessment. Key features include:

- **Anomaly Detection:** Identifying unusual patterns in transaction data to flag potential fraud.
- **Risk Scoring:** Assigning risk scores to transactions based on historical data and patterns.

5.3.1 Implementing Fraud Detection Models

- **Building an Anomaly Detection Model:** Step-by-step instructions for creating an anomaly detection model using Amazon SageMaker.

6. Advanced Machine Learning Techniques

6.1 Natural Language Processing (NLP)

Natural language processing (NLP) enables machines to understand and interpret human language. AWS provides various services for NLP, including:

- **Amazon Comprehend:** A natural language processing service that uses machine learning to find insights and relationships in text.
- **Amazon Lex:** A service for building conversational interfaces using voice and text.

6.1.1 Implementing NLP with Amazon Comprehend

- **Analyzing Sentiment:** Instructions for using Amazon Comprehend to analyze sentiment in customer feedback.

6.2 Computer Vision

Computer vision technologies allow machines to interpret and process visual data. AWS provides several services, including:

- **Amazon Rekognition:** Used for image and video analysis, enabling facial recognition, object detection, and scene analysis.

6.2.1 Implementing Computer Vision Applications

- **Building a Facial Recognition System:** Step-by-step guidance on using Amazon Rekognition for facial recognition applications.

7. Security and Compliance in Machine Learning

7.1 Data Privacy Considerations

When working with machine learning, especially in sensitive sectors like healthcare and finance, data privacy is critical. Best practices include:

- **Anonymization:** Anonymizing data to protect user identities while still allowing for analysis.
- **Compliance with Regulations:** Ensuring that data usage complies with regulations such as GDPR and HIPAA.

7.2 Security Best Practices

To secure machine learning models and data, organizations should implement the following best practices:

- **IAM Policies:** Use IAM policies to control access to ML models and data.
- **Encrypting Data:** Implement encryption for data at rest and in transit using AWS KMS.

8. Monitoring and Optimizing ML Models

8.1 Continuous Monitoring of ML Models

Once a model is deployed, continuous monitoring is essential to maintain performance and reliability. Key practices include:

- **Performance Metrics:** Track metrics such as accuracy, precision, and recall to evaluate model performance.
- **Feedback Loops:** Establish feedback mechanisms to gather data on model predictions and improve future iterations.

8.1.1 Setting Up Monitoring for ML Models

- **Using CloudWatch for Monitoring:** Instructions for using Amazon CloudWatch to monitor ML model performance.

8.2 Model Retraining and Updates

Over time, models may require retraining to maintain accuracy. Best practices include:

- **Scheduled Retraining:** Implementing schedules for retraining models based on new data.
- **Automating the Retraining Process:** Using services like AWS Lambda to automate model retraining when new data becomes available.

9. Real-World Case Study: Implementing Machine Learning for Customer Insights

9.1 Overview of the Company

This case study examines how a marketing analytics company implemented AWS machine learning services to gain customer insights and enhance targeted marketing efforts. Key objectives included:

- **Improving customer segmentation.**
- **Enhancing marketing campaign effectiveness.**

9.2 Data Architecture and Initial Challenges

Discuss the initial data architecture and challenges faced:

- **Siloed Data Sources:** Customer data was scattered across various systems, complicating analysis.
- **Inefficient Segmentation Processes:** Manual segmentation processes were time-consuming and prone to errors.

9.3 Implementing Machine Learning Solutions

Detail the machine learning solutions implemented, including:

- **Centralizing Data in S3:** Migrating customer data to Amazon S3 for centralized storage.
- **Using SageMaker for Segmentation Models:** Leveraging Amazon SageMaker to build and deploy customer segmentation models.

9.4 Results and Lessons Learned

Summarize the outcomes of the machine learning implementation:

- **Improved Customer Insights:** Enhanced understanding of customer behavior led to more effective marketing strategies.
- **Increased Efficiency:** Automated segmentation processes reduced manual effort and errors.

10. Conclusion

In this chapter, we explored the critical aspects of machine learning and AI in AWS. We covered key AWS services for building machine learning models, best practices for implementation, real-world case studies demonstrating successful applications, and strategies for ensuring data security and compliance. Understanding and applying these concepts are essential for organizations looking to leverage the power of machine learning and AI in the cloud.

In the next chapter, we will focus on **"Cost Management and Optimization in AWS,"** discussing strategies and tools to monitor and optimize AWS costs while maintaining performance and scalability.

Chapter 15: Cost Management and Optimization in AWS

Overview

Effective cost management and optimization are crucial for organizations leveraging AWS cloud services. With the flexibility and scalability of the cloud comes the responsibility of managing expenditures to ensure that resources are utilized efficiently. This chapter will delve into strategies, tools, and best practices for managing and optimizing costs in AWS. We will explore key AWS services that assist in cost management, analyze common cost drivers, and provide actionable insights for organizations to achieve cost-effective cloud operations.

1. Understanding AWS Pricing Models

1.1 Pay-As-You-Go Pricing

AWS operates on a pay-as-you-go pricing model, allowing organizations to pay only for the resources they consume. This model provides flexibility and is ideal for dynamic workloads. Key aspects include:

- **No Upfront Costs:** Organizations can start using AWS services without significant initial investments.

- **Scalability:** Costs automatically scale with usage, enabling organizations to adapt to changing demands.

1.2 Reserved Instances and Savings Plans

To help organizations manage costs more predictably, AWS offers Reserved Instances (RIs) and Savings Plans:

- **Reserved Instances:** Offer significant discounts (up to 75%) for committing to a specific instance type for a one- or three-year term. There are two types of RIs:
- **Standard RIs:** Provide the most significant discount for a commitment to specific instance types.
- **Convertible RIs:** Allow changes to instance types during the term but offer lower discounts compared to Standard RIs.
- **Savings Plans:** A flexible pricing model that provides savings on usage across various services (like EC2, Fargate, and Lambda) in exchange for a commitment to a specific amount of usage over a one- or three-year period.

1.3 Spot Instances

AWS Spot Instances allow customers to bid on unused EC2 capacity at substantial discounts compared to On-Demand pricing. This pricing model is suitable for:

- **Flexible Workloads:** Applications that can tolerate interruptions, such as batch processing or data analysis tasks.
- **Cost-Conscious Operations:** Organizations looking to optimize costs without compromising on the required compute resources.

2. AWS Cost Management Tools

2.1 AWS Cost Explorer

AWS Cost Explorer is a powerful tool that enables users to visualize and analyze their AWS spending over time. Key features include:

- **Cost and Usage Reports:** Detailed reports that provide insights into spending patterns and resource usage.
- **Forecasting Capabilities:** Ability to forecast future costs based on historical usage data.
- **Filtering and Grouping:** Users can filter and group data by service, tags, and accounts to gain deeper insights.

2.1.1 Using Cost Explorer

- **Accessing Cost Explorer:** Step-by-step guidance on how to access and navigate Cost Explorer.
- **Creating Custom Reports:** Instructions for creating and saving custom reports to track specific costs.

2.2 AWS Budgets

AWS Budgets allows organizations to set custom cost and usage budgets that track their spending against defined thresholds. Key functionalities include:

- **Alerts and Notifications:** Users can receive alerts when costs exceed budget thresholds or are forecasted to exceed budgets.
- **Multiple Budget Types:** Organizations can create budgets for costs, usage, reservations, or savings plans.

2.2.1 Setting Up AWS Budgets

- **Creating a Budget:** Step-by-step instructions for creating and managing budgets in AWS Budgets.

- **Configuring Alerts:** Guidance on setting up alerts to notify stakeholders of budget thresholds.

2.3 AWS Cost and Usage Reports

AWS Cost and Usage Reports provide detailed information about resource usage and costs, enabling organizations to perform in-depth analysis. Key features include:

- **CSV and Parquet Formats:** Reports can be generated in different formats for easier analysis in data processing tools.
- **Integration with BI Tools:** Users can integrate these reports with business intelligence tools for enhanced reporting and visualization.

2.3.1 Generating Cost and Usage Reports

- **Configuring Reports:** Instructions for setting up and configuring AWS Cost and Usage Reports.
- **Analyzing Data:** Techniques for analyzing cost data using external BI tools like Tableau or Microsoft Power BI.

3. Analyzing Cost Drivers

3.1 Understanding Resource Utilization

To optimize costs effectively, organizations must understand their resource utilization patterns. Common cost drivers include:

- **Underutilized Resources:** Instances or services that are running but not being used to their full capacity, leading to unnecessary costs.
- **Idle Resources:** Resources that are provisioned but not actively being used.

3.2 Tagging for Cost Allocation

Implementing a tagging strategy allows organizations to allocate costs effectively and track spending by projects, teams, or departments. Key practices include:

- **Consistent Tagging:** Establish a consistent tagging structure across AWS resources.
- **Cost Allocation Tags:** Use cost allocation tags to categorize resources and enable detailed cost tracking.

3.2.1 Implementing Tagging Strategies

- **Creating Tag Policies:** Guidance on creating policies for tagging resources in AWS.
- **Using Cost Allocation Tags:** Instructions for enabling cost allocation tags in AWS Billing and Cost Management.

4. Cost Optimization Strategies

4.1 Rightsizing Resources

Rightsizing involves selecting the optimal resource sizes to meet application requirements without over-provisioning. Best practices include:

- **Monitoring Usage Metrics:** Regularly review CloudWatch metrics to analyze resource utilization patterns and adjust instance sizes accordingly.
- **Using AWS Trusted Advisor:** A service that provides real-time guidance to help provision resources following AWS best practices, including cost optimization recommendations.

4.2 Implementing Auto Scaling

Auto Scaling enables organizations to automatically adjust the number of running instances based on demand, helping to optimize costs. Key strategies include:

- **Configuring Scaling Policies:** Set up policies that trigger scaling actions based on CloudWatch metrics, such as CPU utilization or network traffic.
- **Using Scheduled Scaling:** Automatically adjust the capacity of applications during predictable traffic patterns (e.g., scaling up during business hours).

4.2.1 Setting Up Auto Scaling

- **Creating Auto Scaling Groups:** Step-by-step instructions for creating and configuring Auto Scaling groups for EC2 instances.

4.3 Leveraging S3 Storage Classes

Amazon S3 offers various storage classes to help organizations optimize costs based on access patterns. Best practices include:

- **Lifecycle Policies:** Automatically transition objects to lower-cost storage classes based on data access patterns.
- **Intelligent-Tiering:** Use the S3 Intelligent-Tiering storage class to automatically move data between frequent and infrequent access tiers based on changing access patterns.

4.3.1 Configuring S3 Lifecycle Policies

- **Creating Lifecycle Rules:** Instructions for setting up S3 lifecycle rules to manage data storage costs effectively.

5. Monitoring and Reporting Costs

5.1 Continuous Cost Monitoring

Establishing a continuous cost monitoring process is essential for tracking spending and identifying anomalies. Key practices include:

- **Using CloudWatch:** Set up CloudWatch dashboards to monitor cost-related metrics in real-time.

- **Automating Reports:** Automate the generation of cost reports using AWS Lambda and other AWS services.

5.2 Setting Up Alerts and Notifications

To proactively manage costs, organizations should set up alerts and notifications for cost thresholds. Key strategies include:

- **Creating Cost Alarms:** Use AWS Budgets and CloudWatch to set up alarms for budget thresholds and usage limits.
- **Integrating with Notification Services:** Use Amazon SNS to send notifications to stakeholders when cost thresholds are breached.

5.2.1 Configuring Alerts

- **Setting Up Alarms in AWS Budgets:** Step-by-step instructions for configuring alerts in AWS Budgets and CloudWatch.

6. Real-World Case Study: Cost Optimization in a SaaS Company

6.1 Overview of the Company

This case study examines how a SaaS company successfully optimized its AWS costs while maintaining performance and scalability. Key objectives included:

- **Reducing overall cloud expenditure by 30%.**
- **Improving resource utilization without impacting user experience.**

6.2 Architectural Overview and Initial Challenges

Discuss the initial architecture of the company's application, highlighting areas of inefficiency and cost overspending:

- **Over-Provisioned Resources:** Initial deployment had EC2 instances with excess capacity that led to unnecessary costs.

- **Inefficient Data Storage:** Data was primarily stored in standard S3 storage class, resulting in higher costs for infrequently accessed data.

6.3 Cost Optimization Strategies Implemented

Detail the cost optimization strategies employed, including:

- **Rightsizing and Auto Scaling:** Conducted a comprehensive review of resource utilization, implementing rightsizing and auto-scaling for EC2 instances.
- **Implementing S3 Lifecycle Policies:** Transitioned infrequently accessed data to S3 Glacier, reducing storage costs.
- **Regular Cost Monitoring:** Established a cost monitoring process using AWS Budgets and Cost Explorer to track spending and identify anomalies.

6.4 Results and Lessons Learned

Summarize the outcomes of the cost optimization initiatives, highlighting:

- **Cost Reduction:** Achieved a 30% reduction in overall AWS spending while maintaining performance.
- **Improved Resource Utilization:** Enhanced resource efficiency and responsiveness to changing traffic patterns.

7. Future Considerations for Cost Management

7.1 Evolving AWS Pricing Models

As AWS continues to evolve, organizations should stay informed about new pricing models and offerings that could impact their cost management strategies. Key considerations include:

- **New Services and Features:** Regularly review new AWS services that may provide cost-saving opportunities or enhanced performance.

- **Pricing Innovations:** Keep an eye on pricing innovations from AWS that could lead to better cost efficiency.

7.2 Continuous Improvement

Cost management is an ongoing process that requires continuous improvement. Best practices include:

- **Regularly Reviewing Budgets:** Conduct periodic reviews of budgets to adjust for changes in business objectives and resource utilization.
- **Adapting to Changes:** Be flexible and ready to adjust cost management strategies based on business growth and technological advancements.

8. Conclusion

In this chapter, we explored the essential aspects of cost management and optimization in AWS. We covered AWS pricing models, tools for managing costs, strategies for optimizing resource utilization, and real-world case studies that demonstrate successful cost management practices. Understanding and applying these concepts are vital for organizations to effectively manage their AWS expenditures while maximizing the benefits of cloud services.

In the next chapter, we will focus on **"Advanced Networking and Security in AWS,"** discussing strategies for securing cloud networks and protecting data in transit and at rest.

Conclusion

As organizations continue to embrace cloud computing, the journey towards effectively leveraging the vast capabilities of platforms like Amazon Web Services (AWS) becomes ever more crucial. This book has explored a comprehensive range of topics, from foundational concepts to advanced strategies for optimizing AWS usage.

Throughout our exploration, we've seen how AWS provides powerful tools and services that enable organizations to innovate, scale, and transform their operations. However, with great potential comes the responsibility to implement best practices and maintain a focus on efficiency, security, and cost-effectiveness.

Key Takeaways

1. Understanding Cloud Fundamentals

A solid understanding of cloud computing fundamentals lays the groundwork for successful cloud adoption. Key concepts such as the shared responsibility model, pricing structures, and the significance of data security are critical for any organization looking to migrate to or operate in the cloud.

2. Building a Secure and Scalable Architecture

Designing a secure architecture in AWS requires careful consideration of networking, identity management, and compliance. By leveraging AWS services like VPC, IAM, and AWS WAF, organizations can create environments that not only meet performance requirements but also adhere to security best practices.

3. Harnessing the Power of Data

Data is often referred to as the new oil, and AWS offers robust services for data management and analytics. Understanding how to store, analyze, and derive insights from data using services like Amazon S3, Amazon Redshift, and Amazon Athena enables organizations to make informed decisions and drive business growth.

4. Leveraging Machine Learning and AI

The potential of machine learning and artificial intelligence in driving efficiency and insights is profound. AWS provides a suite of services that simplify the implementation of ML and AI solutions, empowering organizations to harness data for predictive analytics, automation, and enhanced user experiences.

5. Cost Management and Optimization

Managing costs effectively is paramount for sustainable cloud operations. By understanding AWS pricing models and utilizing tools like AWS Cost Explorer and AWS Budgets, organizations can gain visibility into their spending, identify cost drivers, and implement optimization strategies to reduce unnecessary expenditures.

6. Continuous Improvement

The cloud landscape is ever-evolving, and organizations must remain agile and adaptable. Regularly revisiting strategies, adopting new AWS services, and ensuring compliance with changing regulations are essential for maintaining operational excellence.

Looking Ahead

As we look to the future, several trends and considerations will shape the AWS landscape:

- **Serverless Architectures:** The shift towards serverless computing with AWS Lambda and other serverless services is likely to continue, offering organizations more flexibility and reduced management overhead.
- **Multi-Cloud Strategies:** Organizations may increasingly adopt multi-cloud strategies to avoid vendor lock-in, enhance redundancy, and optimize costs.
- **Focus on Sustainability:** As awareness of environmental impact grows, AWS and its customers will continue to prioritize sustainable practices, including energy-efficient computing and responsible resource management.
- **Evolving Security Landscape:** As cyber threats become more sophisticated, maintaining a proactive security posture will be paramount. Organizations must stay informed about emerging threats and adapt their security strategies accordingly.

Final Thoughts

In conclusion, the journey of adopting AWS is one of transformation and opportunity. By understanding the key principles outlined in this book and applying best practices in architecture, data management, machine learning, and cost optimization, organizations can harness the full power of AWS to drive innovation and achieve their business goals.

As you continue your cloud journey, remember that the cloud is not just a destination; it's an enabler of business agility, efficiency, and creativity. The tools and knowledge shared in this book are your stepping stones to building a successful and resilient cloud strategy.